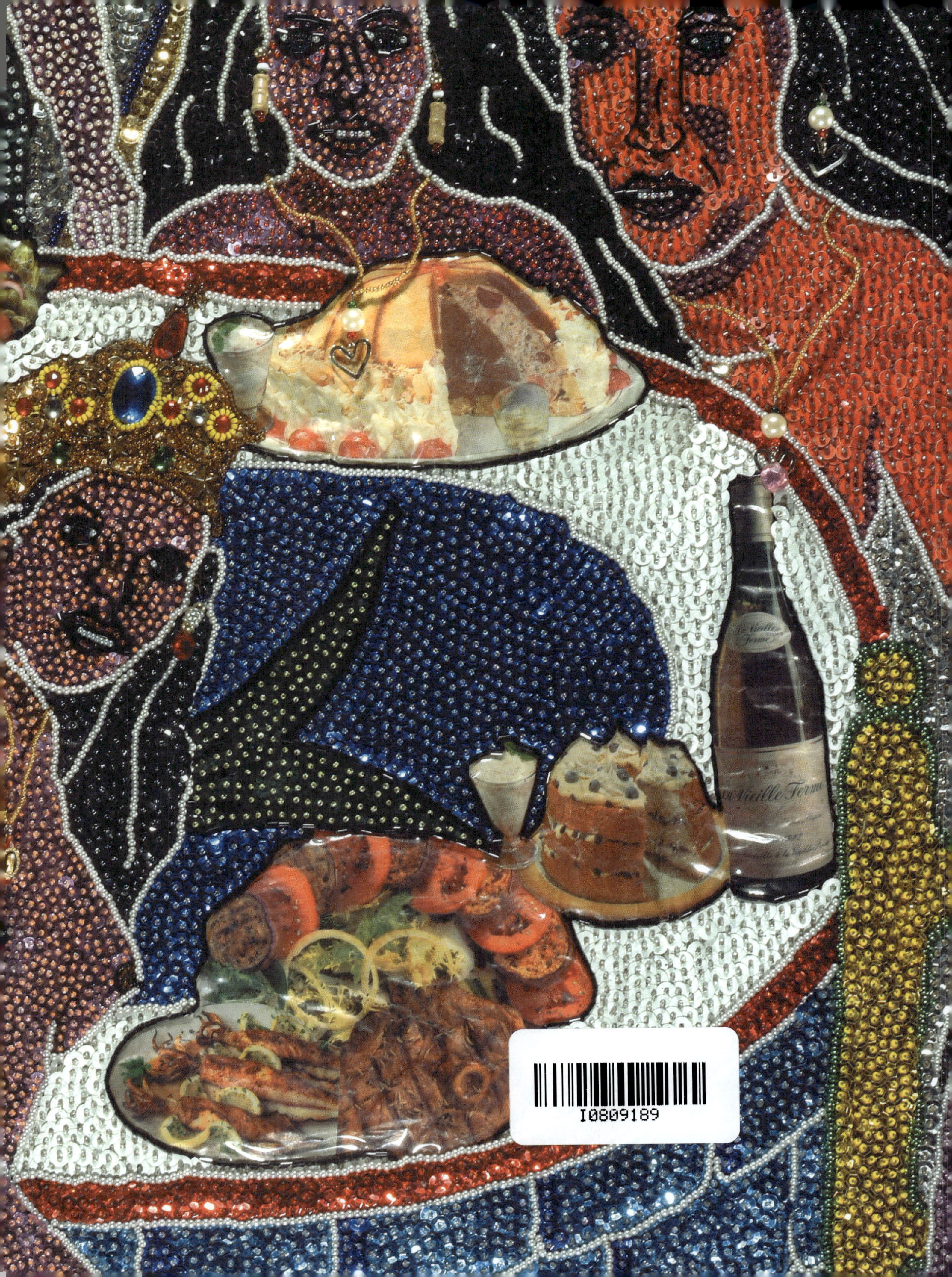
Vieille Ferme

Spirits in Sequins
Vodou Flags of Haiti

Nancy Josephson

Schiffer Publishing Ltd®
4880 Lower Valley Road, Atglen, PA 19310 USA

Library of Congress Control Number: 2006934990

Designed by "Sue"
Type set in ITC American Typewriter/Arrus BT

ISBN: 0-7643-2596-5
Printed in China

Published by Schiffer Publishing Ltd.
4880 Lower Valley Road
Atglen, PA 19310
Phone: (610) 593-1777; Fax: (610) 593-2002
E-mail: Info@schifferbooks.com

For the largest selection of fine reference books on this and related subjects, please visit our web site at **www.schifferbooks.com**
We are always looking for people to write books on new and related subjects. If you have an idea for a book please contact us at the above address.

This book may be purchased from the publisher.
Include $3.95 for shipping.
Please try your bookstore first.
You may write for a free catalog.

In Europe, Schiffer books are distributed by
Bushwood Books
6 Marksbury Ave.
Kew Gardens
Surrey TW9 4JF England
Phone: 44 (0) 20 8392-8585; Fax: 44 (0) 20 8392-9876
E-mail: info@bushwoodbooks.co.uk
Website: www.bushwoodbooks.co.uk
Free postage in the U.K., Europe; air mail at cost.

Contents

Artist and houngan (priest of Vodou) Andre Pierre.
Croix de Bouquet, Haiti 2004
Photo by Ted Frankel

Acknowledgments

While in Haiti I had the privilege of meeting the living treasure, Andre Pierre. He was both a powerful priest of the Vodou religion and one of the most revered painters in all of Haiti. During this meeting Monsieur Pierre talked and sang about his life and philosophy. I came away from this encounter with gems.

Andre explained that there are four articles in life. The first is water. From water all life forms and develops. It is the essence of newborn life. The second article is air. I thought that this meant air as in "we need to breathe." He explained that we need the air to be calm, not just to breathe, but to breathe with relaxation and appreciation.

I was ready for the third article. I just knew it was: earth. Well, when he told me what the third article was I thought my limited Creole skills had vanished completely. I thought he said, "Salt." I countered with, "Don't you mean earth?" Thankfully he was a very patient man. "No," he explained, "Salt. We need salt for spice." Needless to say this little jewel of information set my head reeling.

This book is salt! I try to infuse the writing with devotion, beauty, humor, and well, salt. My effort to thank all the spirits through offerings for guidance and influence is paramount to my life and work.

"Honor and respect" is the greeting one gives before going into a Vodou temple. This book is my attempt at throwing down the salt in honor and respect. To all the spices manifested as people that have made my life and work a continual sumptuous feast, my deepest respect and love.

Obeisance to those who paved the way: Tina Girouard, Katherine Dunham, Milo Rigaud, Karen McCarthy Brown, Maya Deren, Virgil Young, Sondra Thomas, Pierre Monosiet, Marianne Lehman, Donald and Henrietta Cosentino, Sallie Ann Glassman, Elizabeth McCalister, Phyllis Galembo, Maggie Steber, Sue Thomas, Axel Liautaud, Chantal Regnault.

Respect and prayers to those on the ground: Georges Rene, Jean Marie Bien Aime, Marie Cassise, Richard and Lunise Morse.

To those who have gone on: Andre Pierre, Pierrot Barra.

To those who make the search a fruitful and fun treasure hunt: Nancy Forrest, Laurie Beasley from Ridge Art Gallery, Sal Scalora, Kurk Lyons, Ed Gessner, Judy Hoffman, Alden Smith, Bob Corbett, Michael and Michelle Zwack, Nancy Mickelson, Judy and Dick Donovan, Cammie, Chawne and Kent at the Waterloo Art Center, Tony Fisher and Devi Cholet at Indigo Art Gallery, Nicole Smith at Nicole Gallery, Laurie Carmadie at Galerie BonHeur, Bill Bollendorf at Galerie Macondo, Katherine Kean at TapTap and Crowing Rooster Arts, Andy Antippas at Barrister's Gallery, Reynald Lally and Christiane Bourbon from Bourbon-Lally Galerie, and Ted Frankel at Sideshow.

To Carson Zullinger who patiently made this work come alive with his photographic skills.

To Nancy Schiffer and those at Schiffer Books who allowed this book to live.

To my traveling buddies who witnessed it: Maggie Roche, Ted Frankel, and Nancy Hild.

There are no words that can capture the gratitude I feel towards two who have shaped how I've approached this project and, by extension, my work in Haiti. My love and eternal thanks to Marilyn Houlberg: teacher, mentor, shopping sister, and friend. Second, Dr. Jacques Bartoli: a most helpful, open, and kind person who has led me through this potentially treacherous path with tremendous knowledge, grace, and clarity.

To Sylva who opened my eyes.

To David, Jake, and Ruth who opened my heart.

This book is dedicated with love to the memory of my father, Benjamin Josephson, who taught me to be open to the world.

To the artists I give my deepest gratitude and respect.

Oh, by the way, the fourth element is fire.

Introduction

In most folk traditional art there are those upstarts who dare to push at the boundaries of the status quo. Whether the creative urge, spiritual insistence, artistic vision, individual ego or mercenary reality is a work (or whether all of these elements and more play into this stew) there are individuals who rise to the top of their profession. Their work is so stylistically unusual (pirouetting where a simple polka would do!) that it is made instantly recognizable. Their artistic imagery transforms the ordinary into powerful and remarkable symbols of creative ingenuity. The artists represented here have risen above the level of fine artisans and have erased the line where craft meets art. With the gods in their fingers these inspired people transform lowly materials into a joyful expression of living with the spirits. These flag makers have catapulted themselves out of the realm of artisan into a category of internationally recognized artists by virtue of their commitment and success at expressing their individual artistic spark.

The need to keep the hierarchical power system managed enables the continuation of the acceptance of "primitive" work being the only work that could possibly be done by the uneducated Haitians. The notion of sophisticated, nuanced work is inherently threatening as this elevates the standing of the artistic and, by extension, community structure. To look at work by people other than what we categorize as "artist" and throw it casually into the realm of "primitive" is not only dismissive but also missing the deep connections within the work. We do the artist and ourselves a disservice. In addition, most Haitians have been equally dismissive of artistic individuation. Separate voice shakes the internal hierarchy as well.

These artists are by no means primitive. Though they may not have had the educational training and art background that our society values, they perhaps take a larger risk than most by daring to create. The absolute necessity to be able to sell one's work is a driving force in the mind of the flag makers. Anytime work is produced, it costs the artist money in sequins, cloth, and time. There is no "wiggle room" in that solely making art for art's sake cannot be the only psychological force at work. These artists do not come from privileged backgrounds that can allow them to lean on familial comfort zones. To rise up above the non-stop pressures of the prevalence of poverty is a tremendous feat. To do this with art takes vision, tenacity, and self-determination. These artists have risen out of the hold of obscurity and named themselves. They take risks to add something personal, to shout above the hoards. Their personal satisfaction costs. The stakes are high. The risks are huge. There is no guarantee of a sale, yet they keep risking as they keep creating. In Haiti the poor can't risk anything. Life is lived too close to the bone. Yet these artists courageously gamble, continually making innovations in style, technique, and imagery while knowing they can ill afford to lose.

As the medium pushes into the mainstream, making its way into the global stream of ethnographic art, clear artistic voices do emerge dressed in sequins and spangles. This book presents these master flag makers as individuals rather than anthropological timekeepers. Though many Western art movements are born out of reaction to their predecessors (i.e. Abstraction following Impressionism), the flowering of art flag making is a natural extension of its roots. This art has grown organically in a linear progression rather than in reactive shifts.

The Sacred Arts of Haitian Vodou exhibition mounted by the University of California Los Angeles Fowler Museum of Cultural History planted a strong and enduring seed which will result in the continued exploration of the rich art and cultural life of Haiti. Through its didactic approach, the Sacred Arts exhibition opened the door for further and more in depth focus of the many art forms presented. This book is one of the flowers of that seed.

As a caveat or disclaimer (or to dodge the bullet of not having every artist properly represented here), I present this work as a document that shows what I know. It is filled with information given to me over the course of about ten years of interviewing and observing. I am not an academic or an anthropologist. I am an artist who was drawn to this culture through its artwork and stayed to be overtaken by its spirituality. The personal sieve through which I filter the work is to be taken with a grain of salt. This is all I know.

Additionally, the uneasy intersection of spiritual, artistic, and commercial creates a potentially paradoxical construct. The Western concept of a distinct separation of the three is a phenomenon that insists on keeping barriers up. Why this paradigm continues is to be argued elsewhere, however.

Throughout the book I use the Creole spelling "Vodou" rather than the Americanized "voodoo" which has a negative connotation.

The Hotel Oloffson.
Port au Prince, Haiti
Photo by Ted Frankel

How It Works

So it starts as it always does, on the overpainted white wraparound porch of the Hotel Oloffson, a hotel where you meet everyone you are supposed to meet. The porch attracts a full array of characters—visitors, academics, anthropologists, journalists, writers, students, missionaries, Peace Corps workers, artists, and seekers. The locals represent all in the social order—fixers, politicians, elite of all stripes, guides, drivers, artists. The hierarchy is flexible. It all depends on who's got what you need. Deals are made and remade, angles being worked out over rum punch.

Dr. Jacques Bartoli, Nancy Josephson, Jean Marie Bien Aime, Roland Rockville, and Georges Valris on the Hotel Oloffson porch.
Port au Prince, Haiti 2005
Photo by Ted Frankel

This is where I officially started in Haiti, though I'd been drawn in by the spirit and the art long before. I come to this as an artist, swept into it as a servitor of the Vodou spirits. The power of the art and the spirit come together without missing a beat—sparkling and glittering, inciting the spirit that's beckoned to be closer or at least to be tickled with the expression of love created in their honor.

The combination of bead to sequin, color to pattern, subject to style set the tone for the possibility of a glorious outcome—a fully realized composition flowing with the harmonious melody of an object created by man, touched by the gods. The conspiracy to obliterate the creative spirit is met with the same inescapable necessity for the seed to sprout even in barren soil. Haitian artists exist in the most challenging place on earth and answers misery with jewels. Here I have found orchids in the desert. The intoxication I felt compelled me to investigate this phenomenon further. As direct contact with the spirits spurred me on to create my own offerings, invocations, and enticements, my path intersected the bumpy road of a handful of mortal men and women who took the ordinary and made magic. Miracles exist everywhere. In Haiti some are manifested in sequins. This book will hopefully give you a glimpse of the face behind the magic and a clearer picture of how a specific material is transformed into an individual testament to the power of inspired creation.

Nobody's Perfect

On an early morning on one of the first trips to Haiti I found myself sitting at the bar of a downtown brothel (long story) dressed in a long white dress waiting for one of the two mystic marriages that were to be performed later that day at Sylva's peristyle. The bartender came to take my breakfast order. Thankfully, my friend and translator, Georges Rene, had shown up early. He was a friend of the bartender, who was also the brothel's manager. Georges explained that when not at his managerial position at the brothel this gentleman was also a priest of the Jehovah's Witness. My Western sensibilities reeled at this information. I couldn't find the right pocket to put this information in. When I questioned Georges about how this was possible he explained in two words a new theory that changed my life forever. "Nobody's perfect."

Nuts and Bolts

Vodou, a little history, a little technique

Detail of the Haitian flag by Sylva Joseph.
Marilyn Houlberg Collection
Photo by Nancy Josephson

History shows Haiti first making an appearance during Christopher Columbus' voyage to the new world. He did hit the island in his 1492 voyage, finding the island a beautiful, calm, and potentially prosperous venture with a highly functioning indigenous population of approximately 400,000 Taino (of the Arawak tribe) Indians. Shortly thereafter, the Spanish came to do what they had been doing: colonizing and overpowering the existing culture. The Taino were enslaved to work the gold mines. In a short period of time (about fifty years) this population was essentially annihilated due to the inhumane treatment of the slave owners and the disease brought in from the outside culture.

The Spanish renamed Haiti ("mountainous land" in the Taino language) Hispaniola, or "Little Spain." Due to the valuable trade location, the rich soil that yielded goods highly prized by Europeans (cocoa, cotton, sugar, and coffee), the need for cheap labor was necessary to fulfill high demands. The first importation of black slaves began in the early 1500s.

The French started establishing settlements in the north of the island and displaced the Spanish late in the 1600s. The Spanish ceded the western part of the island to the French, who renamed it Saint-Domingue. During the 1700s the French plantations made this colony one of the richest in the French empire. Though it was very small, it managed to produce 40% of all sugar and 60% of all coffee consumed in Europe. It earned the moniker "the pearl of the Antilles."

By the 1790s, the island's population consisted of approximately 500,000 slaves to about 30,000 white foreigners. Some slaves fled into the mountains where they intermingled with the hidden Tainos. Others committed suicide rather than be held at the mercy of the unconscionable slave owners. But when Toussaint Louverture began organizing a revolt against the French occupiers, another period was set in motion.

The ruling French had no idea that slaves could be organized enough to fight a cohesive battle. The plantation owners had set up a system that they thought prevented the slaves from coming together in any real way. They had separated members of the same tribes and broken apart families. They imposed severe restrictions about how slaves congregated and punished severely those who went against their laws. Toussaint Louverture was a smart, capable organizer who successfully fought battles that eventually led to independence. He was captured by the French while attempting to negotiate an end to the fighting in 1802 and died in a French prison in 1803. Jean-Jacques Des salines then took over (along with Henri Christophe) and led the country's black population into the final war for independence. The Republic of Haiti was officially formed as the first black independent nation on January 1, 1804.

Needless to say, this struck fear into the hearts of the colonial powers. The threat was enormous and horribly frightening to their health and well being—both physical and financial. If revolution could happen in Haiti, then why not in other colonies? This fear led to ostracizing Haiti in every way possible. No trade, no communication, no importing and exporting were possible. The country went through troubled times complete with a succession of rulers. In 1820, Jean Pierre Boyer became president. On his watch he felt that in order to gain recognition by France (and by extension the rest of the world) he needed to agree to the French ordinance that required Haiti to pay 150 million francs to France for retribution for their losses during the struggle. This bankrupted Haiti and essentially mortgaged the country so thoroughly that it would never recover.

Haiti's political structure has been in turmoil ever since, with only brief periods of relative stability. The United States' involvement became more pronounced when it decided it needed a larger influence in the Caribbean, partly due to increased German presence on the island. The United States invaded the island and held control of Haiti from 1911 to 1934. Franklin Roosevelt finally withdrew under his "Good Neighbor" policy. During the U.S. occupation, an army was set up that became the ostensible ruling power's force. This military structure gave birth to what became an elite group of fighters known as the "Tonton Macoute." After a series of coups and military power struggles Dr. Francois Duvalier was elected president in 1957. He effectively used the Tonton Macoute to insulate his power and, in 1964, declared himself president for life. Massive emigration by educated Haitians further led to the increasingly horrendous economic and social conditions. When, in 1971, "Papa Doc" Duvalier died, his power was passed to his son, Jean-Claude. He was nineteen years old and was given the name, "Baby Doc."

Under Baby Doc's regime, the repression and crushing economic problems continued. Corruption was rampant and graft was prevalent. The AIDS epidemic began to be recognized in full force. Additionally, Baby Doc accepted a US directive necessitating a slaughter of all Haitian pigs due to the possibility of a swine flu that the US felt might be an eventual threat to American livestock. When the US repopulated the pig population with US porkers, this led to a tremendous problem. Not only were the pigs enormous by Haitian standards (needing to be fed bought feed rather than rely in existing leftovers), but also they weren't bred for the intense heat of the Caribbean. The peasant population regards the pig as their bank account and when these pigs died they were out of options. By 1986 public discontent finally led to the ousting of Jean-Claude.

Though the removal of Baby Doc was a positive move, the system of government was so compromised that between 1986 and 1991 the rule of political instability was more the law.

Meanwhile, a Catholic priest began making noises that were beginning to look like hope for the Haitian people. Jean-Bertrand Aristide was charismatic and came from the population that he wanted to serve. The people looked to him as a man who wouldn't compromise and would put an end to the continual corruption that was endemic of Haitian politics. The beginning of 1991 looked promising. Aristide won the presidential election with a large majority. But, when a September 1991 military coup brought Aristide down, another dark period enveloped the country. An embargo was levied against Haiti by the US, which used this as an opportunity to attempt at restoring Aristide's power. In a country where poverty is the norm, this embargo effectively acted as an unbelievable punishment to the masses rather than the rulers. In 1994, with US forces ready to invade the island, the military government stepped down, allowing Aristide to return and finish out the remainder of his term. A political ally of Aristide's, Rene Preval was elected the next president in 1995. A falling out between the two men led Aristide to develop a separate political party (Fanmi Lavalas). Irregularities and growing disillusionment with Aristide's actions and inability to make significant change began to fester. Aristide was elected by an overwhelming majority in the next election (in 2000), despite claims of vote fraud and intimidation. Tensions between Lavalas and the opposition parties grew and erupted. In 2004 rebels took control of the town of Gonaive, then Cap Haitien, the second largest city in Haiti. As rebels were poised to march on Port au Prince, Aristide left the country. Aristide claimed the US kidnapped him. The US claims that Aristide resigned.

An interim government was put into place with Gerard Latortue as the leader. In the most recent election Rene Preval re-emerged as the newest president. At the time of writing this book, we wait to see Preval's efficacy.

Throughout Haiti's history as an independent republic, the consistent factors of punishing poverty and exclusion from world access created a culture devoid of the ability to move up past the crushing conditions under which it barely survives. Ninety-seven percent deforestation accounts for the lack of agricultural opportunities and creates additional horrors such as the massive flooding that killed many thousands in the tropical storm season of 2004.

Once the "pearl of the Antilles," Haiti is currently the poorest country in the Western hemisphere with 70% unemployment and 80% living in abject poverty.

Vodou

First and foremost, Vodou is a religion and Haiti is a faith-based society. Vodou is in its essence based in the desire for balance. Some spirits are hotter, fierier. Some are calm and cool. All have flourished and all are needed. The lwa (spirits) are intermediaries representing archetypes who embody a wide range of traits. Divided up into cooler (Rada) or hotter (Petro) spirits (along with a host of others who traverse the places between), the lwa are individual deities who are called upon to assist in helping a practitioner or a community with problems both mundane and cataclysmic. In Haiti there is no dearth of either. In a culture where hardships are commonplace—having intermediaries who take on one's earthly trials is a welcome alternative.

The earthly attributes of each spirit allow the individual or group to work towards emotional and physical well-being. The collective congregation is able to transform itself with the powerful pulse of the group effort, calling for the influence of a particular spirit whose ability to minister, admonish and celebrate, and lend credence to their appearance, while coalescing the community. Ritual formulae are followed with the foreknowledge that at any time all hell can break loose. Spirit possessions toss people around like rag dolls. Inviting the spirits to participate in the festivities is a vital part of the ritual. Through possession lwa will "mount" one of the congregants so that the spirit has the physical presence to interpret problems, admonish those who have strayed or disobeyed, and revel in the power of human contact. Ruckuses filled with life and humor overflow—obliterating veves (geometric spirit invitations) made of flour or coffee grounds meticulously "drawn" on dirt floors.

The houngan (priest) or mambo (priestess) preside over their domain as community leaders who's realm is civic and spiritual. The structure of much of Haitian life is set around the workings of the Vodou community. The temple is the community gathering place. Rooms and small dwellings are built around the peristyle (temple), weaving together social and sacred. There is no line that differentiates between usage-only contexts. People of the community lounge on risers that are areas of intense energy when the spirits are invited in. These are the same individuals that may be taken over by one of the spirits to act as counselors to others during possession.

Slaves were captured from a host of West African countries—all of whom had their own sophisticated religious and social structures. A tradition of flexibility within the religions allowed an easy flow of incorporation of spirits from one nation to another. All of the religions were based in a similar philosophy of animism and ancestral worship, which enabled intermingling of the spirits. If a spirit had power it was welcomed. This easy acceptance and integration of outside cultures' icons proved useful in Haiti.

The Altinet Story

Mia, Marilyn, Georges, and I headed out to Carrefour to try to find Lalanne. We stopped (after an unsuccessful hunt) in Leogane, a town a bit further down the road towards Jacmel at a beautiful wall full of colored chromolithograph inspired murals. Georges and Marilyn had previously met the houngan who presided over the temple so we decided to stop and visit. Jean-Paul Altinet met us in the driveway. He was initially cautious and standoffish, wary of what we wanted. He recognized Marilyn and Georges and let his guard down enough to invite us into the temple. From there, the comfort level grew. He invited us into one of the back djevos (shrine rooms) where we saw an altar filled with objects that (even though many were mundane) formed a sacred shrine. Included in this mélange of material was work by the famous mixed-media artist, Pierrot Barra. We were excited to see Pierrot's work in this sacred context. The small room itself was bathed in the glow of red lighting, giving it an intimate, almost claustrophobic feel. Christmas lights (frequently used in temples) circled the room with twinkling white lights. This setting had such a magical quality to it. Altinet donned a black hat with fringe that covered his eyes. He began exhibiting the clear signs that a possession was in process. After a few minutes he turned to us (obviously in trance) and began speaking in the trance language known as "langaj" (which is similar to the notion of "speaking in tongues"). Well, this was quite an occurrence we were witnessing, but throughout the experience I was thrown from one cultural reality into another. Every once in a while as we were deeply present in what was happening in front of us I'd hear the tune "Rudolph the Red-Nose Reindeer" being played by the computer chip attached to the Christmas lights and I'd start laughing. This wacky overlay of cultures taken in and out of context typifies so much of my experience in Haiti.

Flags

Flags in general are identifiers. They signify what tribe or nation one belongs to. They act to rally the troops. Throughout history, flags, banners, and standards are the symbols under which a society comes together physically and metaphorically. The flag "stands" for who we are. Nations hold their flag high, pledging allegiance.

Within the Vodou community the flag is a sacred ritual object that identifies the hounfour and honors the spirits with whom it is associated. The sparkle of the sequin or mirror used to capture the attention of the lwa started in the temples. Drapo Vodou (sequined sacred flags) are unfurled at the beginning of a ceremony. They are power points that are used for both identification and transformation. When the flags are unfurled it signals the congregants to come to order—the sacred is about to come home to roost. The spirits will soon walk next to (or in) the market woman. The close proximity to such a strong personal spiritual connection is one cornerstone in the power of Vodou.

The intricate dance in which the "reine drapo" or "ko-drapo"(queens of the flags—or flag bearers) weave and turn in formalized cadence (suggesting a bow to the stately quadrille dances of the colonial occupiers) lends an elegant feel to set the tone for the upheaval that will follow.

These beautiful ritual objects captivated anthropologists and tourists. Due to the financial needs of the temple, some of these early flags were sold to collectors. As the flags began to be seen and appreciated by others outside of the religion, more became available. These older flags (used specifically for temple ritual) featured a central iconographic image, or images, surrounded by sequins spaced loosely around the image, allowing the fabric onto which they were sewn to be seen. These flags had fringe on three sides and a rod pocket on top into which a long straight piece of wood or metal could be threaded, enabling the flag to be waved easily and with flair.

Sacred ceremonial old flag. Note sparse sequin use and beadwork reminiscent of West African beading.
Courtesy of Dr. Jacques Bartoli

Sacred ceremonial old flag for Saint Jacques Majeur/Ogoun.
Marilyn Houlberg Collection
Photo by Nancy Josephson

Detail of old Saint Jacques Majeur/Ogoun.
Note missing face where chromolithograph image once was.
Also note the beautiful beadwork on the horse.

Sacred ceremonial older flag.
Featuring a "Mary" image. Note the use of sparse sequins sewn onto the background of the fabric, which enables the flag to freely furl.
Courtesy of Dr. Jacques Bartoli
Photo by Nancy Josephson

Detail of older "Mary" flag.

Detail of older ceremonial flag for Ogou(n) Badagris in the form of Saint Jacques.
Note the tight elegant beadwork, which references West African beading.
Courtesy of Dr. Jacques Bartoli
Photo by Nancy Josephson

Sacred ceremonial older flag with serpents and eggs. This is a flag for Damballah, the ancient life force symbolized by the serpent. Keep this flag in mind while looking at iconography used by Yves Thelemaque in his Damballah flags.
Marilyn Houlberg Collection
Photo by Nancy Josephson

Detail of older serpent and egg flag.

Sacred ceremonial older flag detail featuring Saint Jacques as Ogoun.
Note the embroidered horse with the more stylized work on the Saint's face. The difficulty in getting the small features depicted correctly led to the use of the chromolithograph with plastic overlay to solve this problem.

Rara (Haitian carnival) costume top.
This top has sponges inserted into the back of the material to obtain the 3-D element.
Courtesy of Dr. Jacques Bartoli
Photo by Nancy Josephson

Back to Vodou History

Colonial masters were charged with converting the slaves. The church services were the only places slaves could congregate. The Catholic rituals and symbols were secretly folded into the African religious practices. Both religions shared the common structure that included one highest power (in Vodou this is Bondye) who isn't connected with the day to day trials and tribulations that beset individuals. The various saints and angels that are perceived to be more available addressed peoples' daily problems. This syncretic activity enabled the slaves to build up their arsenal of spirits, which added to their power base.

Thus the pictures of the Catholic saints (chromolithographs) became connected with the spirits needed in Haiti. Stories of the different saints commingled with stories of the elder spirits. The saints' pictures served to present recognizable portraits of the spirits. There was an easy association that developed. For example, the chromolithograph of St. Patrick contained images of snakes. Damballah was the serpent spirit, an elder life force and cool water "Rada" spirit. Therefore, in Vodou, when St. Patrick is seen, one automatically knows this to be a vision of Damballah. It is not, however, as simple as St. Patrick being subsumed by Damballah. It is that St. Patrick and Damballah have an association that maintains and incorporates both, adding to the power structure. This follows with many of the Vodou spirits.

Each spirit is in charge of very specific realms. The archetypal nature finds corollaries in many other religions. The spirits have human foibles as well, some being jealous and impetuous, others quick to strike. They all need to be appreciated for who they are and what they can accomplish. They all expect gratitude for their services as intermediaries. They have favorite offerings and colors that go along with their archetypal nature. As expected, the cooler (Rada) spirits like less spirited colors. The hotter (Petro) spirits want to be surrounded with colors that invigorate them.

The following shows a list of Vodou spirits with their Catholic counterparts along with their favorite colors, offerings, and objects as well as special days over which they preside.

The Lwa

The Catholic Saints' Chromolithographs, Their Vodou Counterparts Attributes, Offerings, Colors, Associated Days, and Objects

Legba: Chromolithograph counterpart: St. Lazarus, St Peter or St. Anthony

Legba is charged with opening the door between the earthly world and the spirit realm. He is the first to be recognized at a ceremony. He is asked by the participants to open the door between the two spheres. His favorite colors are red and white. Keys, crosses, and crutches are the symbols associated with Legba. He comes to a ceremony as an old man limping around the temple. He is called to help if something needs to be found. Additionally he can help with "lost souls." His offerings consist of chicken, bones, sweet potatoes, and plantain.

Saint Lazarus chromolithograph. Depicts Legba in the Vodou pantheon.

Saint Antonio chromolithograph.
Also used in depictions of Legba.

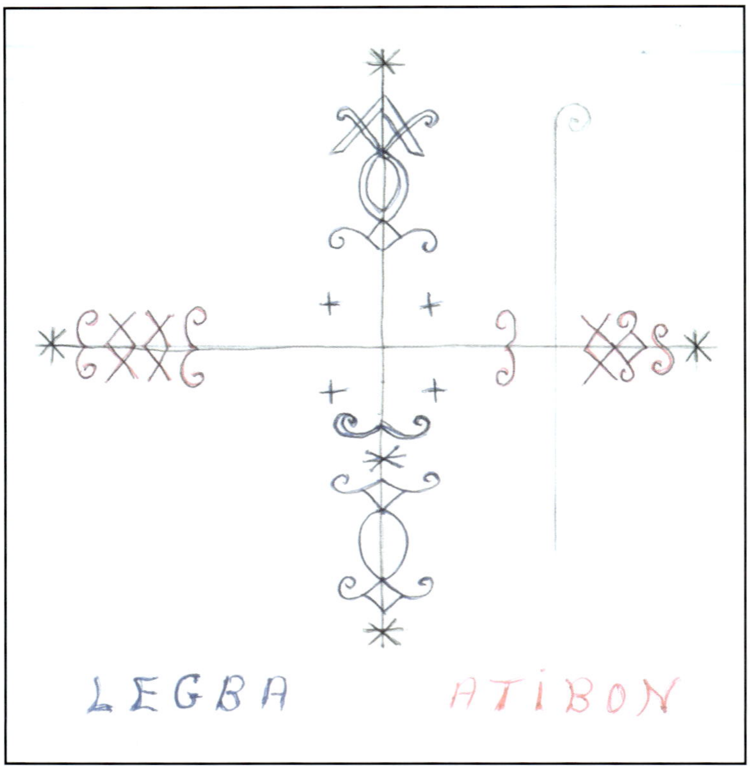

Veve for Legba.
Taken from veve book by Sylva Joseph.
Courtesy of the author
Photo by Carson Zullinger

Sequined veve flag by unknown maker.
The crossroads is also the domain of Legba.
Courtesy of Dr. Jacques Bartoli
Photo by Nancy Josephson

Beaded veve flag by Amina Simeon.
For Legba.
Marilyn Houlberg Collection
Photo by Nancy Josephson

Papa Legba by Roland Rockville.
Note the use of the chromolithograph image of Saint Antonio coupled with the incredible sequin work featuring Rockville's signature "shading." 32" x 36"
Courtesy of the author
Photo by Carson Zullinger

Damballah: Chromolithograph counterpart: St. Patrick

Damballah is a cool, Rada spirit who is a strong, old life force serving as the overseer of wisdom and fertility. He is associated with the serpent. His main offering is an egg, which he slithers over to eat during the course of a ceremony. His favorite color is white. His female consort is Aida Wedo who is seen as the rainbow.

Saint Patrick choromolithograph.
Depicts Damballah in the Vodou pantheon.

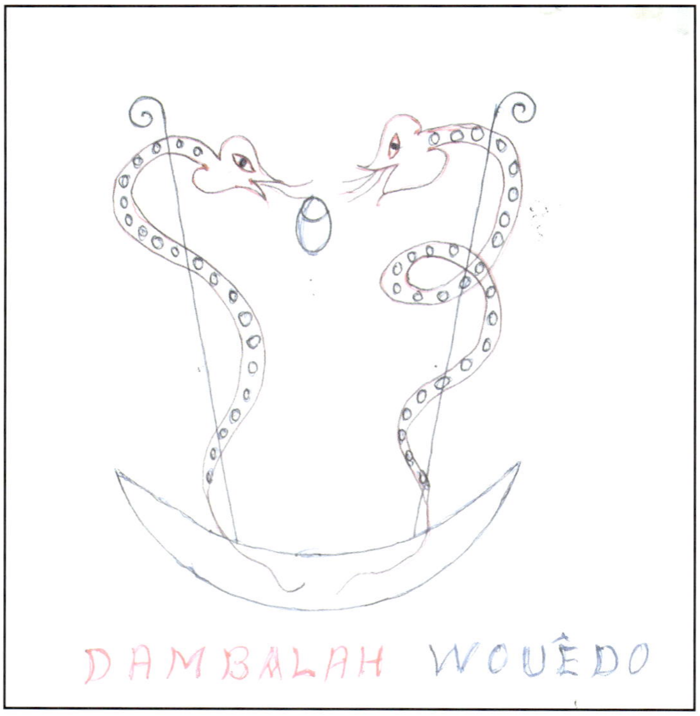

Veve for Damballah Wouedo.
The serpent, Damballah, frequently is coupled with his consort, Wouedo, who is depicted as a rainbow.
From the veve book by Sylva Joseph
Photograph by Carson Zullinger

Damballah Wouedo by Yves Thelemaque.
Collection of Dr. Jacques Bartoli courtesy of Ridge Art
Photo by Nancy Josephson

Dambala veve flag from the atelier (workshop) of Jean Baptiste Jean Joseph.
Courtesy of Judy Hoffman
Photograph by Carson Zullinger

Papa Damballah by Roland Rockville.
Taken from the chromolithograph of Saint Patrick, this flag incorporates Vodou elements such as the prominent serpent exiting the church window.
Courtesy of Dr. Jacques Bartoli
Photo by Nancy Josephson

Saint Patrick/Damballah by Georges Valris.
This flag has many of the typical elements found in flags by Valris such as hearts, fish, and rainbow half circle forms.
Courtesy of Dr. Jacques Bartoli
Photo by Nancy Josephson

Saint Patrick/Damballah by Roland Rockville.
In this small 14" x 14" flag, Rockville needed to use the chromolithograph to show the face of the saint. Note the use of French curves in the border. This is one of Rockville's trademarks.
Private Collection
Photo by Carson Zullinger

Saint Patrick/Damballah by Eveland Lalanne.
Here Saint Patrick is identified as San Patricio. Lalanne learned his trade in the Dominican Republic and frequently uses the Spanish names for the saints.
Marilyn Houlberg Collection
Photo by Nancy Josephson

Marassa: Chromolithograph counterpart: St. Cosmos and St. Damian

The Marassa are the sacred twins who hold a special kind of power. They are deeply associated with their African roots. They are the protectors of children and hold domain over doctoring and medicine. When seen as Marassa Twa (the twins plus one—which includes the child born after the twins), the power base jumps up exponentially. They have been associated with the chromolithograph of the Three Graces who typically represent love, truth, and justice. The Three Graces have also been known to represent three faces of the Erzulie family (Freda, Dantor, and La Siren). These twins, when they come to the ceremony, can be very mischievous and demanding. They are, after all, children, and as such want feasts of candy, popcorn, soda, and toys.

Veve for the Marassa.
Sometimes not only are the Marassa twins represented, but also represented are Marassa Twa (trios). The child born after the twins is said to have even more power than the older siblings.
From the veve book by Sylva Joseph
Photo by Carson Zullinger

Opposite page:
Cosmos and Damian chromolithograph. These two represent the Marassa, or twins in the Vodou cosmology.

Veve flag for the Marassa Twa, or twins plus one.
Maker unknown.
Courtesy of Dr. Jacques Bartoli
Photo by Nancy Josephson

Marassa Twa Veve flag by Georges Valris.
Courtesy of Judy Hoffman
Photo by Carson Zullinger

Marassa Twins by Antoine Oleyant.
This is the work of the artist who took the flag making tradition out of the temple and into the art world.
Courtesy of Tony Fisher and Devi Cholet of Indigo Arts Gallery

Marassa Twa flag by Myrland Constant.
This features the veves and symbols used in Vodou ceremonies honoring the sacred twins.
Marilyn Houlberg Collection
Photo by Nancy Josephson

Marassa twins flag by Maxon Scylla.
Antoine Oleyant's brother-in-law, Maxon, keeps Antoine's designs alive in his depiction of the twins.
Marilyn Houlberg Collection
Photo by Nancy Josephson

Three Graces chromolithograph. Sometimes the Three Graces are seen as the Marassa Twa, sometimes as sisters Erzulie Freda, Erzulie Dantor, and La Siren.

Three Graces by Georges Valris. His trademark background features half circle rainbows along with stars. 33" x 40"
Courtesy of the author
Photo by Carson Zullinger

Three Graces by Roland Rockville. Rockville incorporates the veve diagram in this piece. His signature style of effectively employing the limited color choices in the sequins to "shade" the figures is also evident. 32" x 36"
Courtesy of the author
Photo by Carson Zullinger

Below:
Three Graces by Evelyn Alcide. This heavily beaded flag is an example of the newer technique being used in flag making by women who spent time working at wedding dress making factories.
Courtesy of Tony Fisher and Devi Cholet from Indigo Arts Gallery

Ogoun: Chromolithograph counterpart: St. Jacques, St. George

Ogoun (also Ogou) is actually a family of spirits. Collectively they represent a strong military force of power and protection. Individually they have a wide array of influences. They are the masculine warrior who also oversees the realm of metal and machinery. They are from the hotter (Petro) side of the Vodou pantheon. The chief Ogoun spirits are: Ogoun Feraille, Ogoun Badagris, Ogoun Balindjo, Ogoun Batala, Ogoun La Flambeau. These various incarnations of the family control various specific forces associated with masculine power. Ogoun's color is red. As a warrior, Ogoun is a sword-wielding soldier who loves rum, rice and beans, red roosters, and bulls.

Saint Jacques/Ogoun chromolithograph.

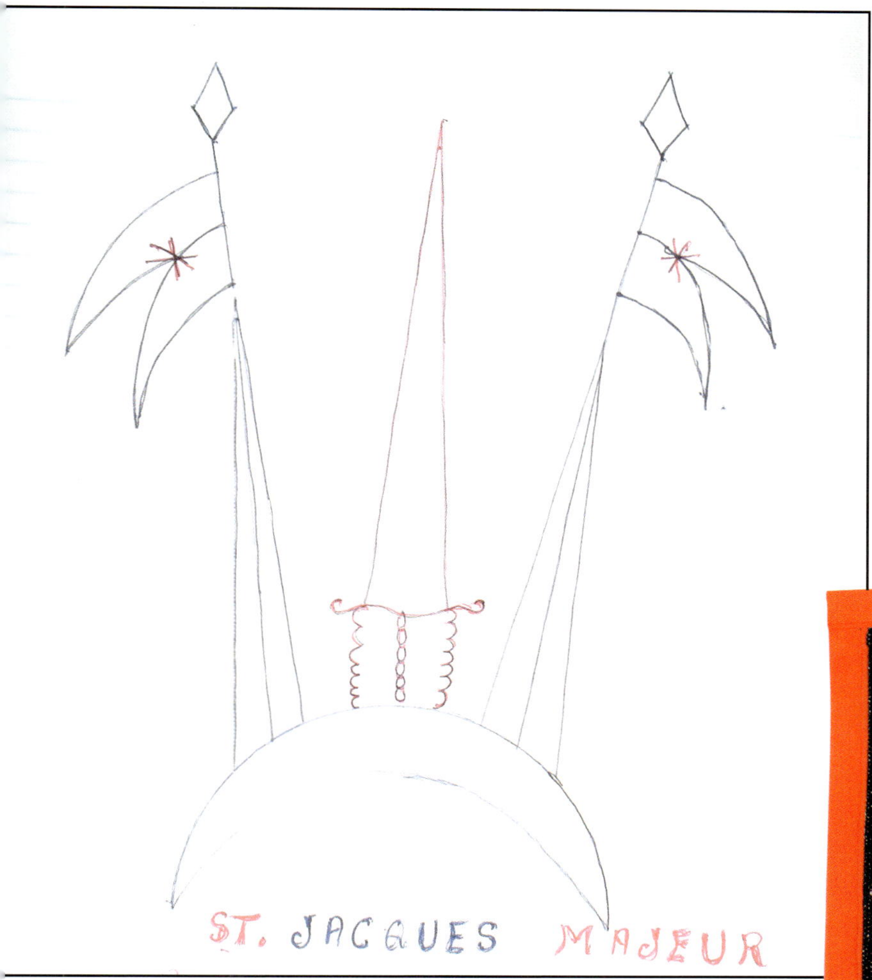

Veve drawing from book by Sylva Joseph.
Courtesy of Nancy Josephson
Photo by Carson Zullinger

Ogoun veve flag by unknown maker.
Courtesy of Judy Hoffman
Photo by Carson Zullinger

Saint Jacques/Ogoun flag by unknown maker.
The fabric tabs attached to the side of the border, along with the sparse sequins, suggest sacred usage for this flag.
Marilyn Houlberg Collection
Photo by Nancy Josephson

Saint Jacques/Ogoun flag by Georges Valris. Cartoon-like figures with his trademark filled up background make up Georges' visual vocabulary.
Marilyn Houlberg Collection
Photo by Nancy Josephson

Saint Georges/Ogoun chromolithograph.

Saint Jacques/Ogoun flag by Yves Thelemaque.
Yves uses the chromolithograph underneath the sequin work to allow the face of the saint to show through underneath a layer of clear plastic sheeting.
Courtesy of Kurk Lyons
Photo by Carson Zullinger

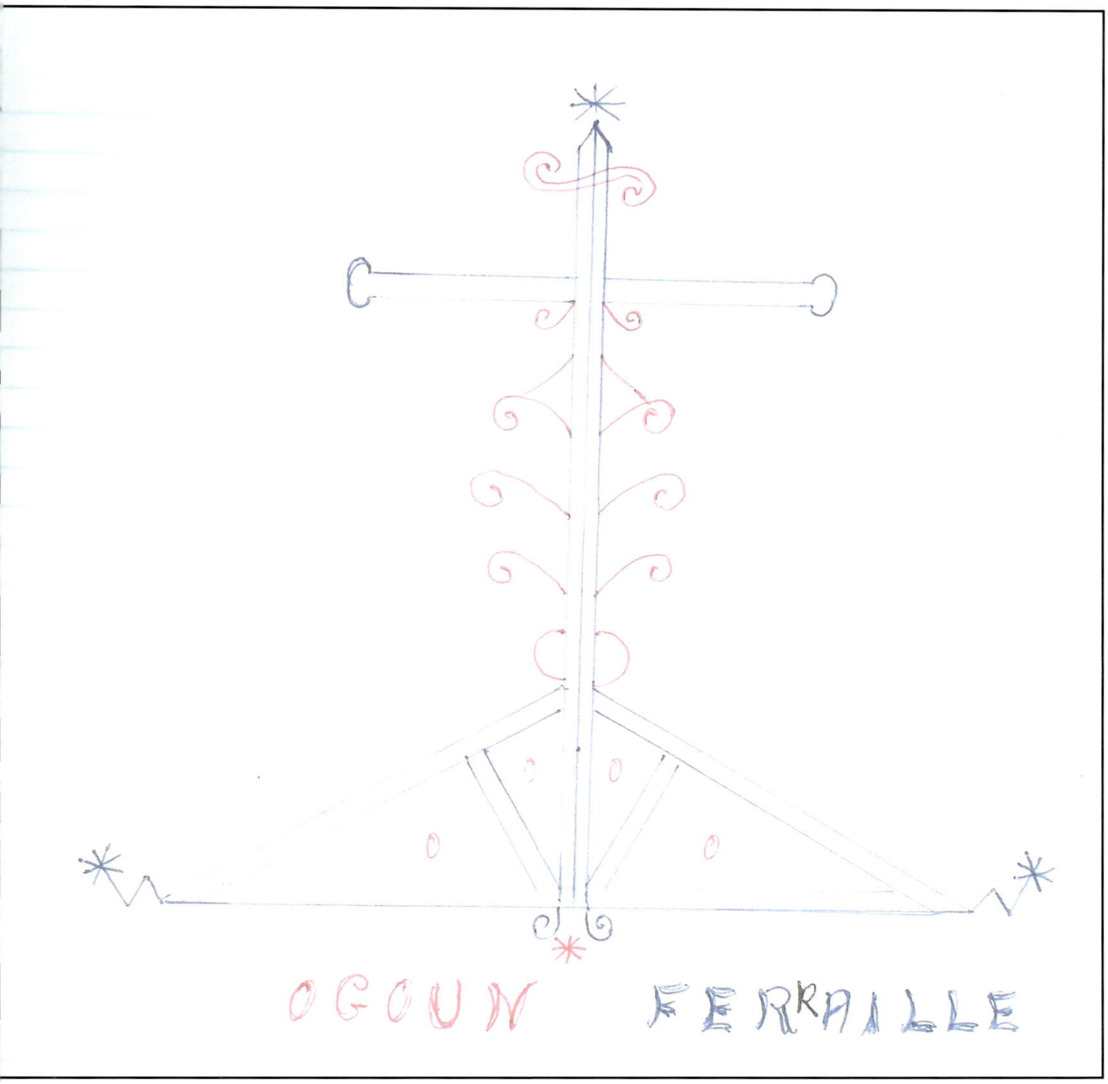

Veve diagram for Ogoun Ferraille by Sylva Joseph.
Courtesy of the author
Photo by Carson Zullinger

Below left:
Ogou(n) flag by unknown maker.
Courtesy of Dr. Jacques Bartoli
Photo by Nancy Josephson

Below:
Saint Jorge/Ogoun flag by Eveland Lalanne.
Note the Spanish spelling used for St. George.
Marilyn Houlberg Collection
Photo by Nancy Josephson

Erzulie Freda: Chromolithograph counterpart: Mater Dolorosa de Monte Cavario

Though Freda is a Rada (cool) spirit, she is known to exhibit high drama during a ceremony. She is abbreviated into the "Goddess of Love," but she also possesses a much more elaborate structure which incorporates rages of jealousy and almost manic-depressive weeping. She is known for her beauty and over the top love for jewelry and perfume. Her offerings include cake, white doves, makeup, and champagne. Her favorite colors are pink and pale blue. She assists in all realms of love, from fertility to lost love.

MARIA DOLOROSA DEL MONTE CALVARIO

Mater Dolorosa de Monte Cavario/
Erzulie Freda chromolithograph.

Veve drawing for Erzulie Freda by Sylva Joseph.
Courtesy of the author
Photo by Carson Zullinger

Erzulie Freda flag from the atelier of Jean Baptiste Jean Joseph. This beautiful flag combines both the beading and sequin techniques.
Courtesy of Judy Hoffman
Photo by Carson Zullinger

Erzulie Freda veve flag by Antoine Oleyant.
Courtesy of Dr. Jacques Bartoli
Photo by Nancy Josephson

Erzulie Freda flag by Eveland Lalanne. Using the Catholic chromolithograph of Mater Dolorosa as inspiration, Lalanne embellishes the figure using tight beadwork to highlight her abundant jewelry.
Courtesy of Dr. Jacques Bartoli
Photo by Nancy Josephson

Erzulie Freda flag by Georges Valris. Sparse sequining in the background doesn't take away from the opulence of material that Freda demands.
Private Collection
Photo by Carson Zullinger

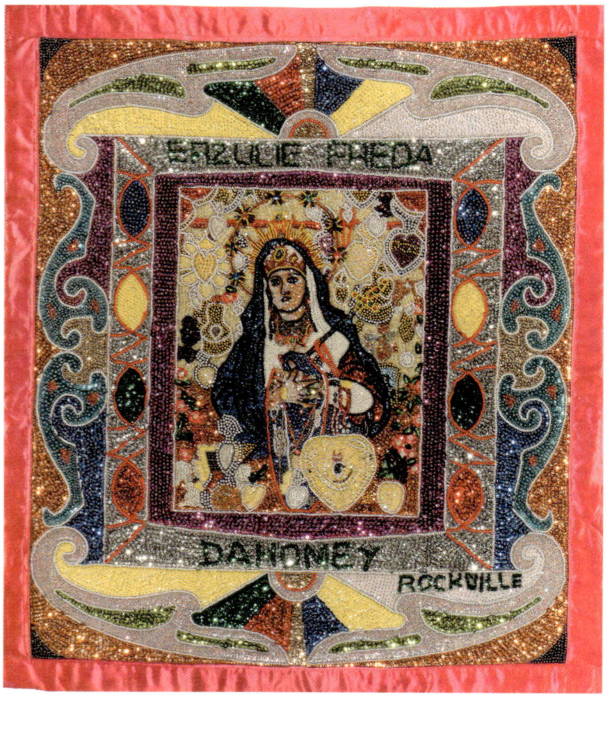

Erzulie Freda by Roland Rockville. Rockville's trademark sequin shading and use of French curves in the borders contribute to the overall beauty of the piece.
Private Collection
Photo by Carson Zullinger

Erzulie Dantor: Chromolithograph counterpart: Our Lady of Czestochowa or Our Lady of Mount Carmel

Erzulie Dantor is the hot, Petro side of the Erzulies. As such, she is cruder and tougher than her Rada counterpart. She is a dark skinned market woman who puts up with nothing. Her independent spirit and rough exterior serve her well in Haiti. She oversees the realm of the maternal, fiercely protective of her children and, by extension, all children. She is also said to be a lesbian. She is said to have been scarred on her cheek by the sister, Freda, during a fit of jealous rage. Dantor's favorite offerings include a black pig, unfiltered cigarettes, and rum or strong sweet wine. Her colors are red and blue (often together).

Our Lady of Czestochowa/Erzulie Dantor chromolithograph.

Veve diagram for Erzulie Dantor by Sylva Joseph.
Courtesy of the author

Veve flag by atelier of John Baptiste John Joseph.
The combination of both bead and sequin work suggest this atelier's own signature.
Courtesy of Judy Hoffman
Photo by Carson Zullinger

Erzulie Dantor by unknown maker.
This wonderful, quirky piece shows a stylized but solid spirit.
Courtesy of Maggie Roche of Edge Art
Photo by Nancy Josephson

Erzulie Dantor by Yves Thelemaque. This shows Yves' early borders stepping away from, but still referencing, a more standard border treatment. Vodou iconography abounds.
Courtesy of Dr. Jacques Bartoli
Photo by Nancy Josephson

Erzulie Dantor by Georges Valris. There is no reference of Vodou iconography in this work done by a devout Catholic who makes Vodou flags.
Courtesy of Dr. Jacques Bartoli
Photo by Nancy Josephson

Erzulie Mapiangue chromolithograph.

Veve for Erzulie Mapiang (also spelled Mapiann), who is viewed as Dantor's little sister.
Courtesy of Judy Hoffman
Photo by Carson Zullinger

Mapiann flag by Amina Simeon. Amina takes this depiction straight from the chromolithograph, using beads as her artistic medium.
Marilyn Houlberg Collection
Photo by Nancy Josephson

La Siren: Chromolithograph counterpart: Nuestra Senora de la Caridad or St. Martha

La Siren is sometimes seen as another in the Erzulie family. Depicted as a mermaid, she is the mother of the ocean, both strong and powerful. She can be calm and instills her devotees with graceful force. As her Petro counterpart, Labalenn (or the whale), she can also be a very overwhelming force of nature, able to destroy with the power of the flood and hurricane. She is the spirit of musicians—an artistic muse. She is frequently seen in her depictions with a comb, a mirror, and some form of musical instrument. She loves shells, fish, and all things of the sea. Her sacred color is blue. La Siren's consort, Agwe, is the king of the sea. He is depicted as a sea captain, complete with military garb. His Catholic counterpart is St. Ulrich (who holds a fish in the chromolithograph).

Nuestra Senora de la Caridad/La Siren chromolithograph.

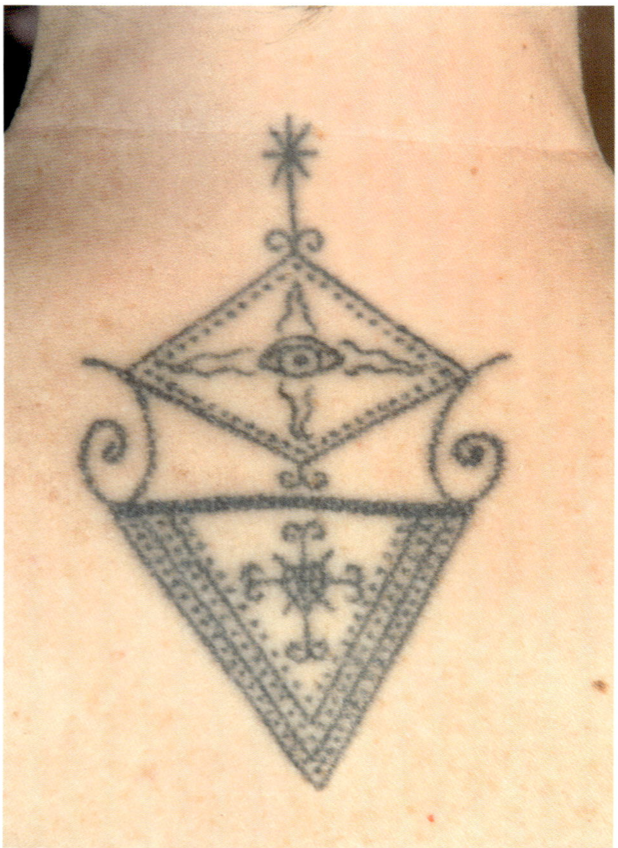

Veve tattoo for La Siren.
From neck of author

La Siren by Antoine Oleyant.
Fish are used to break up the central image.
From the collection of Dr. Jacques Bartoli
Courtesy of Laurie Beasley of Ridge Art
Photo by Nancy Josephson

La Siren by Georges Valris.
Once again Georges fills the background with a host of images and patterns.
Marilyn Houlberg Collection
Photo by Nancy Josephson

La Siren by Roland Rockville.
Here La Siren is set in a calm environment where she can contemplate her surroundings and her own image in the mirror.
Marilyn Houlberg Collection
Photo by Nancy Josephson

La Siren by Ronald Gouin.
Refereces to Antoine's La Siren indicate how much Gouin as Antoine's student took in as his own vocabulary.
Courtesy of Dr. Jacques Bartoli
Photo by Nancy Josephson

Saint Ulrich/Agwe chromolithograph.

Saint Ulrich/Agwe by Eveland Lalanne.
The image comes directly from the chromolithograph, with the added signature Lalanne treatments, including use of a wide variety of beads and sequins.
Courtesy of Dr. Jacques Bartoli
Photo by Nancy Josephson

Agwe by Yves Thelemaque.
This features iconography associated with the powerful sea captain.
Courtesy of Laurie Beasley of Ridge Art
Photo by Nancy Josephson

Agwe by Georges Valris.
Here Georges fills in the background with fish faces all looking at the main character.
Courtesy of Dr. Jacques Bartoli
Photo by Nancy Josephson

Bossou: Chromolithograph counterpart: St. Vincent de Paul

Bossou is the earth. He is shown as a bull. In the agricultural world on which Haiti relies he has a strong, aggressive hold on the land. His favorite colors are red and black.

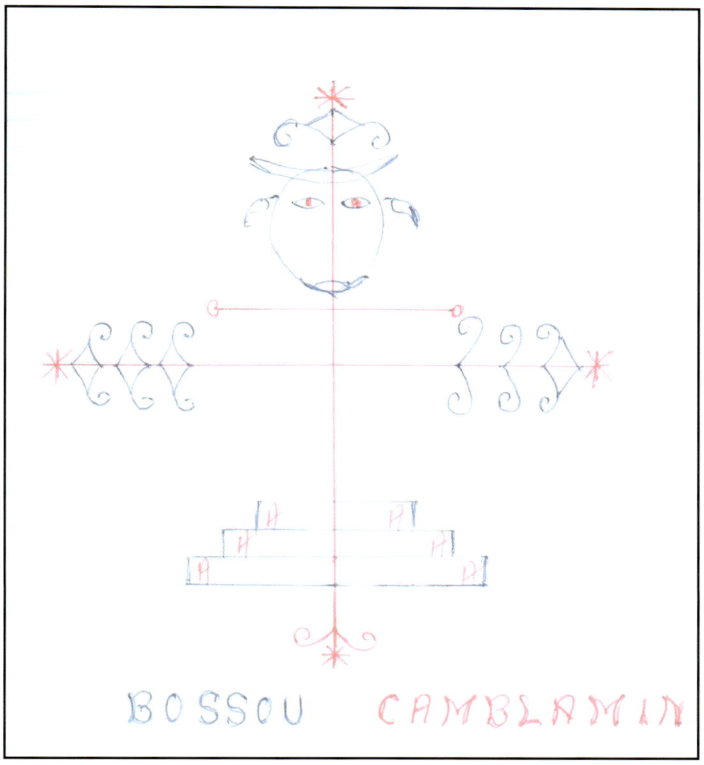

Veve diagram for Bossou by Sylva Joseph.
Courtesy of the author
Photo by Carson Zullinger

Bossou flag by Ronald Gouin. Here Gouin's name is almost as large as the spirit for whom this flag was made.
Marilyn Houlberg Collection
Photo by Nancy Josephson

Couzin Azaka: Chromolithograph counterpart: St. Isidore

Couzin Azaka (also known as Papa Azaka or Zaka) is the farmer. He tends the soil as the patron of agriculture. When he comes to the ceremony, he likes to be dressed in denim, take his pipe and straw bag, go into a corner, and eat quickly. He is a gentle, unsophisticated peasant. His colors are blue and red and his favorite offerings are rice and beans, tobacco, sugar cane, and kleren (Vodou moonshine).

Saint Isidore/Azaka chromolithograph.

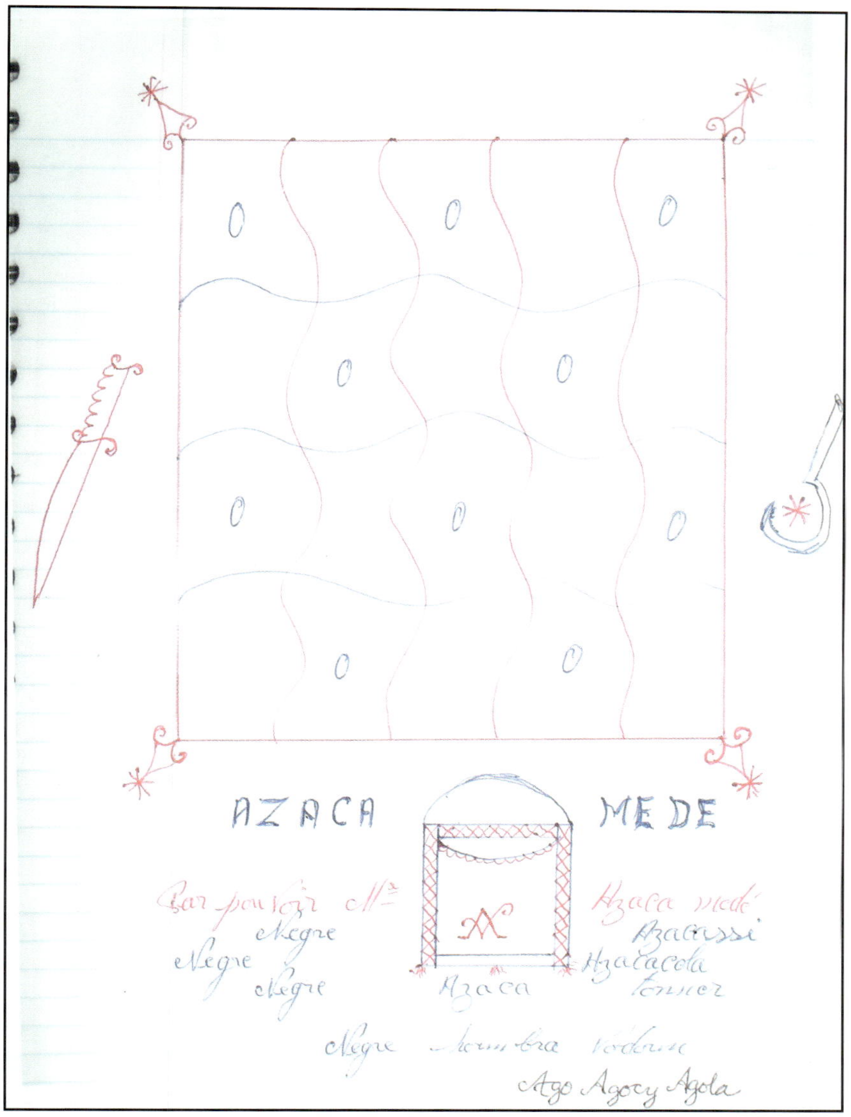

Veve diagram for Azaca Mede/Couzin Azaka by Sylva Joseph.
Courtesy of the author
Photo by Carson Zullinger

Below left:
Couzin Zaka by Yves Thelemaque.
This features the chromolithograph image of Saint Isidore alongside of Vodou objects.
Courtesy of Dr. Jacques Bartoli
Photo by Nancy Josephson

Below:
Couzin Zaka by Amina Simeon.
Here Azaka is featured with his signature pipe, macoute (straw bag), and bottle of kleren (raw liquor).
Marilyn Houlberg Collection
Photo by Nancy Josephson

Saint Isidore/Azaka by Yves Thelemaque.
In this flag, Yves goes all out with his elaborate border work along with a beautifully sequined image of the saint.
Courtesy of Kurk Lyons
Photo by Carson Zullinger

Couzin (Ạzaka)/Saint Isidore by Amina Simeon.
This diminutive piece (8" x 10") packs a lot of tightly rendered work into a small space. It is a tribute to the fine craftsmanship of Amina's atelier.
Private Collection
Photo by Carson Zullinger

Gran Bwa: Chromolithograph counterpart: St. Sebastian

Gran Bwa is depicted as part tree, part human. Overseeing the realm of the forest, Gran Bwa knows medicinal secrets that he shares with those who he is willing to help. He also is one of the overseers of initiation, giving up the last secrets of the priesthood to those deemed worthy. He is strong, tall, and powerful in his roots and leaves. His colors are brown and green.

Grand Bois by Roland Rockville.
The figure is part man, part tree as is the spirit in Vodou. The snake that slithers up the tree is King Damballah, the serpent life force, here depicted with a crown.
Marilyn Houlberg Collection
Photo by Nancy Josephson

Veve for Grand Bois d'Ilet (Gran Bwa) by Sylva Joseph.
Courtesy of the author
Photo by Carson Zullinger

Granbois Ile by Eveland Lalanne.
This stable "crossing guard" overseer is Lalanne's version of the spirit of the forest.
Marilyn Houlberg Collection
Photo by Nancy Josephson

Granbois by Lherison Debreuse.
This flag shows Lherison's technique, which employs a three-dimensional look to the central figure.
Courtesy of Dr. Jacques Bartoli
Photo by Nancy Josephson

Grand Bois Ile by Yves Thelemaque.
A host of Vodou ceremonial objects surround Yves' version of this spirit.
Marilyn Houlberg Collection
Photo by Nancy Josephson

Loko and Aiyzan: Chromolithograph counterpart for Loko: St. Joseph; Counterpart for Aiyzan: St. Lucy

Loko (also known as Papa Loko) and Aiyzan oversee initiation into the priesthood. Loko protects the temple while Aiyzan assists with the initiates. Loko's is depicted as a fighting red rooster. Aiyzan uses her powers to chase away evil during initiation rituals. She is associated with palm fronds and during the end of the initiation ceremony the new serviteurs wear shredded palm fronds over their heads to shade their eyes.

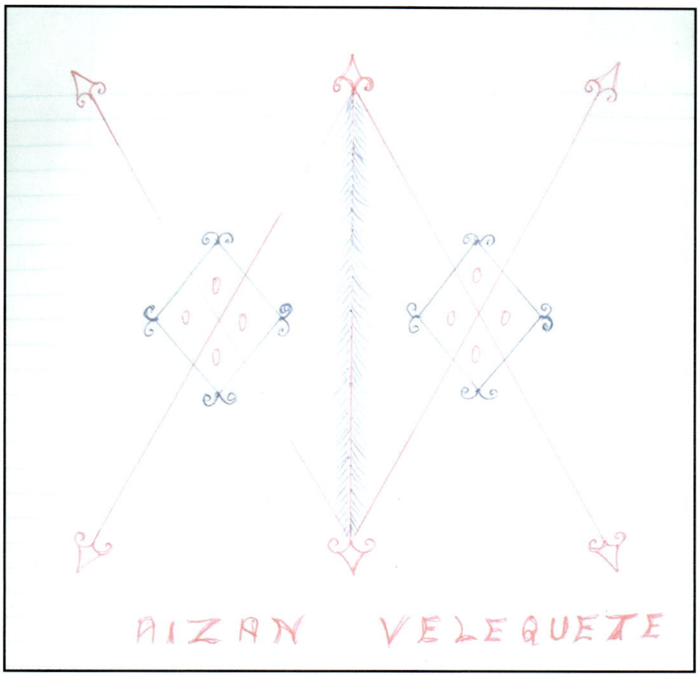

Veve diagram for Aizan Velequete by Sylva Joseph.
Courtesy of the author
Photo by Carson Zullinger

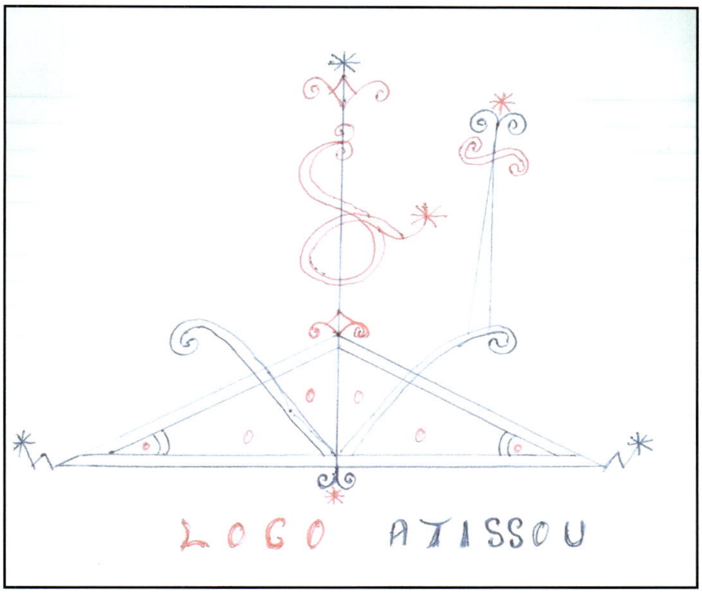

Veve diagram for Loco Atissou by Sylva Joseph.
Courtesy of the author
Photo by Carson Zullinger

Aizan flag by maker "R.M."
Courtesy of Dr. Jacques Bartoli
Photo by Nancy Josephson

Papa Loko by unknown maker.
This is a strong and graphically vibrant veve capturing the spirit of Loko who oversees the temple.
Courtesy of Dr. Jacques Bartoli
Photo by Nancy Josephson

Simbi: Chromolithograph counterpart: Moses

Simbi is the spirit of rain and fresh water. He also is a master magician. In current life his realm includes electricity (which should flow in currents like a river). His colors are white and green.

Simbi Andezo by Yves Thelemaque. This flag features a veve for Simbi, whose realms include fresh water and electricity. *Courtesy of Kurk Lyons* *Photo by Carson Zullinger*

Guede: Chromolithograph counterpart: St. Gerard

Guede (also Gede) is the intermediary between this world and the next. There are many incarnations of Guede (Baron LaCroix, Baron Samedi, Baron Cimetre, and the female counterparts, Gran Brigitte and Marinette) who, like the Ogou family, have specific overseeing duties. Guede is a trickster who loves to come to a ceremony and stir things up. His mischievous, playful, and oft-times bawdy nature can be quite amusing. He is a misunderstood character in that his is the realm of death and the cemetery. As such, he also is seen as a strong doctor and protector of children. Additionally, he oversees rebirth and sexuality. His colors are purple, black, and white. He comes to a ceremony and dons a top hat and sunglasses with one of the lenses popped out (this alludes to the notion of being able to be in between this world and the next). He tells lewd jokes, dances suggestively, and eats and drinks kleren (Haitian moonshine) with tremendous appetite.

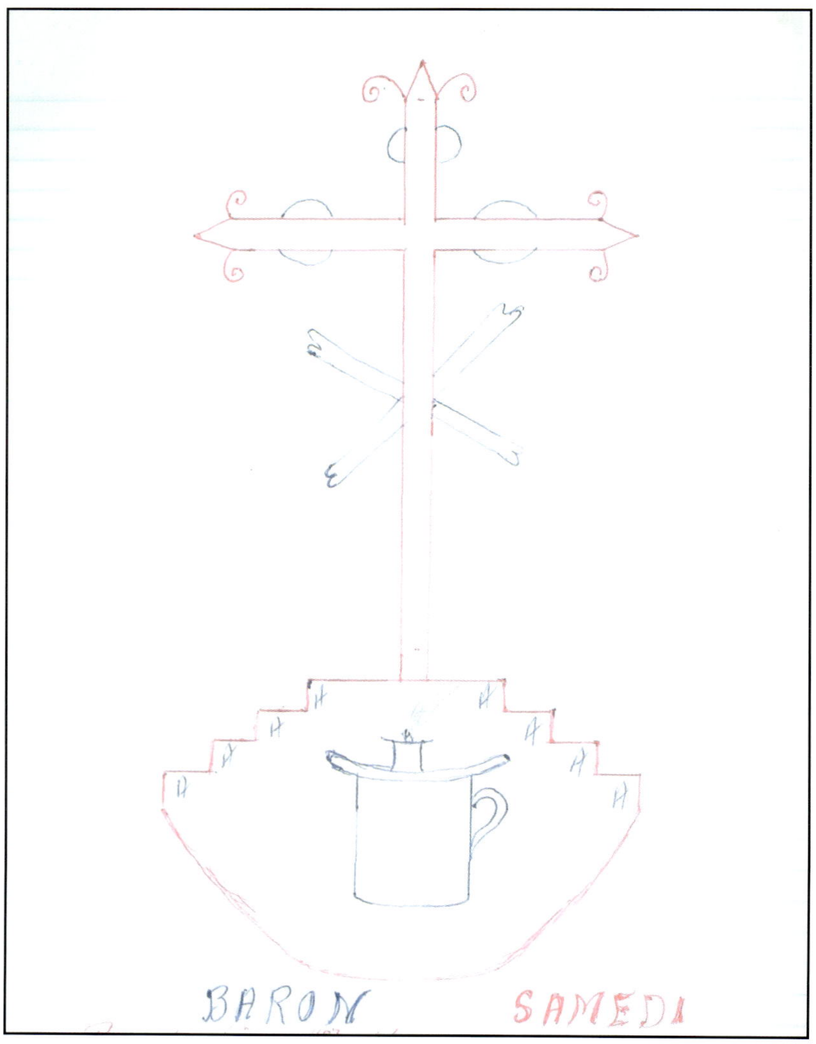

Veve diagram for Baron Samedi (one of the Guede family) by Sylva Joseph. *Courtesy of the author* *Photo by Carson Zullinger*

Saint Gerard/Guede chromolithograph.

Baron LaCroix (Baron of the Cross) by Yves Thelemaque.
This flag shows many of the objects associated with the spirit of the cemetery.
Marilyn Houlberg Collection
Photo by Nancy Josephson

Guede/Saint Gerard by unknown maker.
This flag shows a huge array of objects and iconography coupled with the saint's image.
Marilyn Houlberg Collection
Photo by Nancy Josephson

Guede Rassou Mazaka by Amina Simeon.
This flag visually shows the gravity of the cemetery.
Marilyn Houlberg Collection
Photo by Nancy Josephson

Older ceremonial flag for Guede by unknown maker.
This features the chromolithograph with plastic overlay to show the pieces of the chromolithograph that are difficult to render in sequins.
Marilyn Houlberg Collection
Photo by Nancy Josephson

Baron Lacroix by Eveland Lalanne.
In Lalanne's version of the Guede, skeleton heads float over and around other objects associated with the spirit of the cemetery.
Courtesy of the author
Photo by Carson Zullinger

This list is in no way a complete list of the spirits. There are thousands of lwa who act as intermediaries for every social, financial, and medical situation that exists. For every problem there is a sphere of influence that a Vodouist can come to for help. Making sense of a challenging world where it seems to be impossible to effect any change is made easier if one knows they may be able to go somewhere for help. Comfort in the knowledge that the lwa are able to intercede on the behalf of those who feel at the mercy of their circumstances offers tremendous value to the believer.

Minocan veve by "G.F."
This piece uses bold color to signal the power of all the saints.
Courtesy of Dr. Jacques Bartoli
Photo by Nancy Josephson

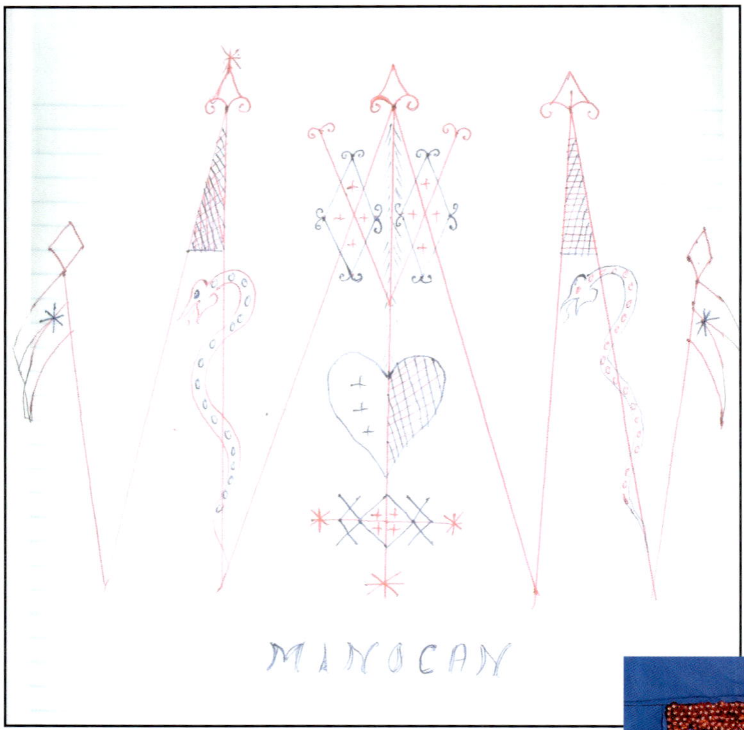

Veve diagram of Minocan or All the Saints by Sylva Joseph.
Courtesy of the author
Photo by Carson Zullinger

Tout les Saints/All the Saints by Georges Valris.
Georges' version of the all-encompassing veve is beautifully rendered with swirls and outlined lines, giving it visual impact.
Courtesy of Tony Fisher and Devi Cholet of Indigo Arts Gallery
Photo by Carson Zullinger

Veves

Each spirit has a veve with which that spirit is associated. Before the ceremony begins, one or more Veve ground drawings (whose concept and design elements come from an amalgamation of indigenous Taino Indian, West African ground drawings, and colonial filigree ironwork) are beautifully, meticulously "drawn" onto the ground in front of the Poteau mitan (center post) in the hounfour (temple). The houngan (priest) or mambo (priestess) carefully guides a powdery substance (traditionally corn meal, coffee grounds, or flour) through his or her fingertips to create the intricate design. The houngan and mambo is versed in the design of all the veves and, depending on their artistic and aesthetic sensibility, produce one or more of these geometric patterns so expertly that the spirit(s) invoked will be enticed to join the ceremony. Veves are essentially invitations to the lwas (spirits) who are honored, necessary participants. During the course of the ceremony these "invitations" are obliterated by the participants who dance over and through the veves to the different drum beats that are also used to entice the lwa to join the festivities. All these movements are performed around the central focus of the ceremony, the Poteau mitan (or poto mitan) that acts as the axis between the earthly and the mystic world.

Technique

Sequined flags are constructed in the following way: First a piece of fabric AND a stabilizing backing material (such a burlap in older flags and plastic rice bags in more recent pieces) are stretched and stapled onto a wooden frame. A design is either drawn onto the fabric before or after stretching. This frame is placed onto sawhorses so that the sewer (or sewers) can put one hand underneath the frame and one hand on top of the fabric. A threaded needle is pushed up through the underside of the material. Each sequin has a central hole through which the needle is pushed. A small seed bead is threaded onto the needle. The needle then goes around the bead and back through just the sequin, then the front of the fabric and through to the underside. This effectively locks the sequin onto the surface of the fabric. Some makers like to outline their designs first in a larger bead. This creates distinct lines, which are then filled in by the sequins. Some makers will use only sequins to demarcate different figures and backgrounds by color only. Occasionally a chromolithograph is attached directly onto the fabric and the maker uses the picture as the design. Because of the detail in the chromolithograph, the maker may decide to use plastic sheeting to cover the part of the chromolithograph that the maker wants to keep exposed. This plastic acts as a window to the design underneath. Saint's hands, face or other very specific elements are difficult to capture with the limited color palette and size of the sequins, so the decision to use the plastic coated chromo as a central part of the design element is a quirky, but useful tool.

When the surface of the fabric has been covered to the maker's satisfaction, the piece is taken off the frame. A backing (normally of satin, but sometimes

Needle comes up and "catches" the sequin.
Photo by Carson Zullinger

Needle pushes from under the frame.
Photo by Carson Zullinger

Needle then goes through bead.
Photo by Carson Zullinger

Needle goes around the bead.
Photo by Carson Zullinger

Bead "locks" the sequin in place and the process continues.
Photo by Carson Zullinger

velvet or patterned cotton) is sewn on using the folded edges of the backing as a border for the finished piece.

Traditionally the flags are approximately either one square yard of fabric or, more recently in the rectangular formatted art flags, 30" x 36". Each requires twenty-five to thirty-six eight-millimeter sequins per square inch. The typical art flag then requires somewhere between 30,000 and 40,000 sequins per piece. Depending on how many sewers are working on a piece, the finished product will be done either in a few days or a week. Since the number of sewers is dependant on the market (how popular is the flag maker's work, is the time period in which they are working before a particularly significant celebration such as Carnival where one can depend on more tourist activity), the atelier (workshop) workers will ebb and flow. The sewers sitting around the frame develop a rhythm to the process, not unlike sewers at a quilting bee. The easy flowing banter and fluid motion of the needle make the time pass relatively effortlessly. Ateliers are frequently located in a covered yard area or on rooftops. Any breeze that can be caught is welcome. Children accompanying their parents play around the frame, sometimes offering freshly threaded needles to the sewers. Though this is a business and expectations of proficiency exist, the overall atmosphere is comfortable.

Going to Sylva's

I arrived at Sylva's one morning to deliver sequins and hang out. He had on a previous trip given me flags to sell so that I could buy sequins in the States and bring them back. The materials that enabled him to make money (sequins) were in short supply these days. Factories that made beaded and sequined garments were closing down, so the availability of the sequins was becoming more of a problem.

Sylva and the others of the house welcomed me. He brought me into the peristyle (temple) where we saluted the four cardinal points (North, South, East, West) with libations. We went into the two back djevos (or bagis-shrine rooms) to salute the Rada and Petro spirits. Once again, Sylva explained what I was required to do at the next juncture of my initiation process. We chatted for a while more as I processed the information. In the time I had spent with Sylva (and in Haiti), one part of my growth into the religion was the acceptance of my limitations as an outsider. The cultural collide that exists was and is a tremendously important piece to contend with. What I can do, and how and when to do it is a constant struggle. My American life and my life in Haiti can sometimes be quite a difficult negotiation. The struggle continues, yet with a much easier overlay. I find Sylva's expectations are perhaps bigger in my mind than his—same as it always is.

I go out to the small open room where a few flags are in various states of completion. I sit with some of the men who are sewing, thread a needle, and start sewing with them. All the younger kids gather around this unlikely scene. Sylva corrects the way in which I sew a sequin onto the border, showing me how to slice the sequin with a razor blade not quite in half to fit the rigid straight line needed for a sharp border. My clumsy attempt (complete with a level of self deprecation) was humorousiy appreciated. After a while I got into the rhythm of the sewing and the kids went to do other things. The "blan" was just another pair of hands for a while.

Flags and the Art World

There are any number of stories that have surfaced about who was most responsible for the flag market's energizing. Most overlap so that the same individuals' names come up over and over. Most notably, the flag makers who are said to have been the most responsible for the first wave of art market flag making were Ceus St. Louis, or "Tibout," and Joseph Fortine, or "Boss To." Both were influenced by the combination of the sacred flags and the colorful sequined and beaded carnival costumes from Brazil they had seen. They were both steeped in the strong Vodou traditions and both became popular figures in Port au Prince. These half brothers were influential artists and priests of the religion. Tibout was the eldest. He took the younger Boss To into his temple and under his wing. Tibout was well known in Port au Prince. His Rara groups (Haitian Carnival) were legendary. His costumed rara troupe was held in high esteem. The position that he held as a maker of beautiful outfits for his group added to his legend. Once he and Boss To saw the sequined Carnival garments of Brazil, they combined their already skillful ideas of rara costumes with the highly embellished costumes of Brazil. The easy transition and natural extension of using the sequins to more fully embellish the flags was inspired. Since Tibout was a Vodou priest and had made temple flags and was well known for his Rara costumes, it's no surprise that he received orders for temple flags. First a mambo that lived and practiced near the Church of St. Anne ordered an Erzulie Freda flag with the request that Tibout use the chromolithograph central image with sequins to surround her. Other orders followed. Other flag makers in the Bel Air area, Sylva Joseph, Edgar Jean Louis, and Clotaire Bazile were among other artists being commissioned to make flags for temple use. As more flags were seen, more were ordered. A market outside of the temple was developing. The fully sequined pieces (as opposed to the partially sequined flags used in ceremony) were becoming sought after by a growing body of foreigners who appreciated these beautiful and unusual objects. With so many artists working around one geographical area, a regional style evolved.

The Bel Air style of flag making developed using some standard forms. Despite obvious commercial competition, these makers frequently sold collaboratively, using one peristyle to sell each other's work.

Sylva Joseph and Edgar Jean Louis

Both Sylva and Edgar have worked out of the same temple for years. Both are well-respected houngan and have their own individual following. This section groups them together because they both essentially follow similar formulae when making a flag. It is a direct extension of old-style flag making, but is fully sequined. The flags were made either using a central iconographic image or veve. Sometimes a stencil was employed to make the central design. These stencils were used by many of the same flag makers in the Bel Air area. A solid sequined background, normally of one color, then surrounded the central figure. This then was bordered with a sequined pattern of either triangles or scalloped half-circles. Occasionally a chromolithograph was laid onto the fabric to use as the central figure and plastic was used to let the face or other significant features of the saint come through.

Their flags are tight, clear, and professionally rendered. Sylva, born in 1930, and Edgar, born in 1921, have put in their time as spiritual and community leaders. They are well-respected and well-loved parts of their communities both in Bel Air as well as their extended families around the world. This family includes the large number of individuals who have been initiated into their Vodou families.

Sylva Joseph.
Photo by Marilyn Houlberg

Baron Lakwa (Baron La Croix/Baron of the Cross) by Sylva Joseph.
This shows clear and crisp iconography in the no nonsense Bel Air style.
Marilyn Houlberg Collection
Photo by Nancy Josephson

Sobo Bader (Bade) by Sylva Joseph.
A direct veve with Sylva's signature old school scalloped border.
Courtesy of Ann and Ed Gessen
Photo by Carson Zullinger

Erzulie Freda by Edgar Jean Louis.
Edgar uses the chromolithograph under the sequins with plastic overlay to let Freda's features come through.
Courtesy of Waterloo Center for the Arts
Waterloo, Iowa
Caribbean/Haitian Collection

Saint Jacques/Ogoun by Edgar Jean Louis. Edgar once again uses plastic to its best advantage. The flag also uses the Bel Air scalloped border.
Courtesy of Judy Hoffman
Photo by Carson Zullinger

Postal stamp by Edgar Jean Louis. The plastic, usually used to let the saint's features show through, here allows the face of Aristide to be visible.
Courtesy of Dr. Jacques Bartoli
Photo by Nancy Josephson

Detail of postal stamp flag by Edgar Jean Louis.

Jacques Bartoli

Doctor Jacques Bartoli came from a prominent Port au Prince family. His father was a well-known and equally well-respected doctor who, among other things, was responsible for establishing free medical clinics in Haiti. The father expected the son to follow in his footsteps. Although Jacques had artistic sensibilities and aesthetics, he became a doctor.

Though personal challenges curtailed his medical career, his love of art endured. His interest in architecture helped in turning his land in the Pacot area of Port au Prince into a multi-tiered apartment complex where both foreigners (settled in for the long haul or there for a brief stint) and Haitians are welcomed. The gregarious open-door spirit of the place acted (and continues to be utilized) as a safe harbor for any number of journalists, UN workers, artists, Peace Corp folks, and others to interact comfortably. Jacques is responsible for setting the tone. He has continued to work within the medical community as well as co-founding (with childhood friend, Dr. Aldi Castor) the Haitian Resource Development Foundation, which is responsible for facilitating projects such as construction of self-sustaining fresh water purification stations in remote areas of Haiti.

Through his connections with artists coming through his building, he became engaged in the artwork of Haitian artists. Over the course of several years I have come to know Jacques as a friend, facilitator, collector, organizer, and constant champion of his beloved Haiti. As this flag book became a reality, I focused our interviews on his stories about the flags and how he came to build one of best flag collections in the world.

Dr. Jacques Bartoli.
Photo by Nancy Josephson

Jacques' Story

Sondra Thomas was a diplomat's wife. Her husband worked at the US embassy. The US had a connection with the Musee D'Art Haitien. With Sondra's appreciation of art, she began working in the Musee gift shop in the late 1970s. Her aesthetics were drawn to the beauty of the flags. Artists were always hanging around the plaza on which the Musee stands trying to sell their work. Foreigners would come to the Musee to buy local art and crafts. Sandra encouraged the making of the flags and would buy or take consignments from those

Gran Bwa by Joseph Oldof Pierre.
Oldof's Gran Bwa shows the half tree, half man figure over the brule zin (flaming cauldron) which symbolizes an activation of power. Also note Oldof's leafy vine, which contains the central figure.
From the collection of Laurie Beasley, Ridge Art
Photo by Laurie Beasley

Guede by Joseph Oldof Pierre.
This flag shows not only Oldof's use of his signature leafy vines but also fills the picture plane with a panoply of other symbols, including veves, cross, coffin, skeleton head, and an image of Bossou (the bull).
Courtesy of Dr. Jacques Bartoli
Photo by Nancy Josephson

La Siren by Joseph Oldof Pierre.
Here La Siren is featured as the patron of musicians as well as the mistress of the sea.
37" x 29"
Courtesy of the author
Photo by Carson Zullinger

who came by. As the support increased, so did the supply. Additionally, Pierre Monosiet, director of the Musee (a knowledgeable and capable man who had tremendous curatorial skills and supported Haitian art), appreciated the flags as well as other art and objects. Flag makers Antoine Oleyant and Oldoff (Joseph Oldof Pierre, 1955-1994) both acknowledged the encouragement and support by Sondra Thomas as an impetus to keep developing their artistic skills and producing flags. At this time Antoine was making and selling woodcarvings to tourists in the plaza outside the Musee. Antoine had also learned the flag sewing techniques in the temple.

Jean Marie Bien Aime was also a force in the market. He acted as a liaison between artists, the Musee, and other interested buyers. He set up shop in front of the Musee and flag makers and other artists would leave their wares with Jean Marie. Sondra relied on Jean Marie to translate the flag imagery to potential clients.

Meanwhile, photographer and photojournalist Maggie Steber had developed friendships with any number of artists and Vodouists. She was a tenant in one of Jacques' apartments. Since she was interested in objects she saw in the temples, she was offered things to buy. She essentially is in a large way responsible for establishing an easy market for the flags and other Vodou related items. She was an important proponent for the artists who loved and appreciated her. Her friendship with Antoine led to her giving Jacques money to oversee Antoine's health issues. Jacques met Edgar Jean Louis when Edgar came up to the apartment compound to see Maggie. Jacques befriended Edgar, who opened the door for Jacques' knowledge of the Vodou world. Jacques was not collecting flags at this point, but he had visitors who were interested in the flags. He would buy flags as small gifts for friends and would act as facilitator if a friend wanted to buy flags. Because they were Maggie's friends, Edgar and Antoine were the main artists with whom Jacques associated. Then other artists started coming to call. Jacques began buying more flags to help out the artists, figuring he could give the flags as presents to friends.

In 1987 a friend and writer, Jeanette Tagert, came to Jacques looking for a project. Jacques encouraged her to write about the flags, which were becoming more and more popular with visitors. Since Jacques had the entré into the temples as well as the trust of the artists, the writer solicited Jacques' help with the research. The research started with Edgar taking Jacques up to the Bel Air section of Port au Prince. Boss To was invited over to Edgar's house. He and Jacques sat and Boss To told him what he knew about the flags and other things.

Jean Marie Bien Aime.
Photo by Ted Frankel

Boss To

Boss To told Jacques about learning how to play baseball from the American soldiers during the US occupation that ended in 1929. Spitballs and curveballs dotted the conversation. He told of a big Rara event that took place in the 1950s in the large stadium. Tibout and his Rara group were invited to participate in the event as part of the entertainment. Tibout's group was to dance and play music. Towards the end of their performance a wooden table was brought out. Tibout lifted the table with his teeth. The crowd loved this. Then, a little girl was put on top of the table and again Tibout lifted the table with his teeth. The crowd went wild. Tibout's popularity catapulted itself into legendary status.

Back to 1987

Jacques' friend, Jeanette, gave up the book project, but many connections had already been made and much of the research had just gotten off the ground. As luck (and the spirits) would have it, this valuable information would find itself put into the right hands.

Tina Girouard (a well respected and well-known artist in her own right) was the president and organizer of the Festival International de Louisiane in Lafayette, Louisiana. Tina would only take on this huge responsibility if Haiti was included in the festival. She valued the influence the island had in the Francophile based celebration and took a stand that it too should be represented. She invited Haiti to participate in the 1987 festival, but got no response from the Department of Tourism. Her friend, Dr. Aldi Castor (Jacques' boyhood friend and fellow co-founder of the Haitian Resource Development Foundation), was enlisted to help facilitate Haiti's participation. Aldi called Jacques, who agreed to assist in finding the right group and helping coordinate the enormous obstacles of getting visas for the group and organizing the travel arrangements from Haiti. During this time period, Jacques and Tina spoke often and developed their own friendship. During the festival a mutual friend, Jeanette (Tagert), flew to Lafayette. With her, she had a gift for Tina. It was a small flag made by Yves Telemaque. As Jacques describes it, Tina "got it" right away.

In 1989, Tina received a commission to create several large banners for the Lafayette airport. She used this opportunity to employ the sequined flag techniques and worked with flag maker Yves Telemaque long distance on this project.

Richard Morse

Richard Morse is the manager of the magical Oloffson Hotel. Raised in the States by a Haitian mother and an American father, he grew up virtually unaware of his Haitian culture. His mother had been a famous singer and a spectacular beauty. His father was an academic.

His position is an interesting one since he is literally of both cultures and chose to live in Haiti. He has the (perhaps unenviable) ability to be a fly on the wall—able to get an overview while traversing the slippery slope of interior politics and policies.

As a musician, Richard was drawn to Haiti looking for the Vodou rhythms. He came to Haiti for the first time in 1985. Having an association with the hotel enabled him to work and support himself while on his quest. Previously Richard had worked in the art and business world and recognized the idea that the two worlds combined created a positive synergy and piqued interest level. At that time different hotels hosted folkloric shows for their guests. Monday night was the Oloffson's night. Traditional dance and singing was featured.

Eventually, as manager of the hotel, Richard pushed the art and business worlds further together. He had met the influential, talented, and deeply committed Maggie Steber. Maggie's connections with the artists and Richard's musical affinity were recognized and valued by both. "Maggie is the kind of person who I would do anything for." As a trusted proponent and friend to Antoine, "When she said, 'Work this deal out' (with Antoine) I said, okay." "This deal" meant that Richard would lease a section of the hotel courtyard out to Antoine. The deal was struck with an agreement that Antoine would pay for the space in flags. Since the Oloffson is like a magnet for foreigners of all stripes, this agreement would prove terrifically important in getting Antoine's work recognized in the outside world.

Richard also supported other artist by mounting shows with collectors and ex-pats such as Bill Brictson and Selden Rodman. Initially he wasn't particularly interested in the flags. When he saw his first flags, he thought the lines were "crooked and that they were funny." When he met Eveland Lalanne and saw his work, Richard thought differently. So, when Maggie brought up the suggestion of opening an atelier with Antoine, the pump had already been primed.

Richard remembers Antoine being very hands on in his atelier—stretching the cloth, drawing, choosing the colors of the sequins, and sewing. After Antoine's tremendous success at the Lafayette festival, Antoine was interested in growing his business. Richard remembers Antoine wanting to branch out and make t-shirts and other tourist crafts. Since Richard was disinterested in this idea, Antoine moved his atelier to an area near the Prince Hotel.

Richard continues to run the hotel. His band, RAM, plays at the Oloffson every Thursday night and satisfies his first love, music. They have built up an international reputation and have become a significant force in the world music scene. Having found out that his mother was a mambo has deepened Richard's roots to the Vodou community. He went through his own initiation to become a Vodou priest and currently practices the religion in a deeply spiritual way. Additionally he has become a flag designer and, with the assistance of Mona, a former sewer for Antoine, produces his own flags.

Puritan Vodou by Mona.
Richard Morse's band, RAM, used this flag as the cover for one of their CD's.
Marilyn Houlberg Collection
Photo by Nancy Josephsonb

1990

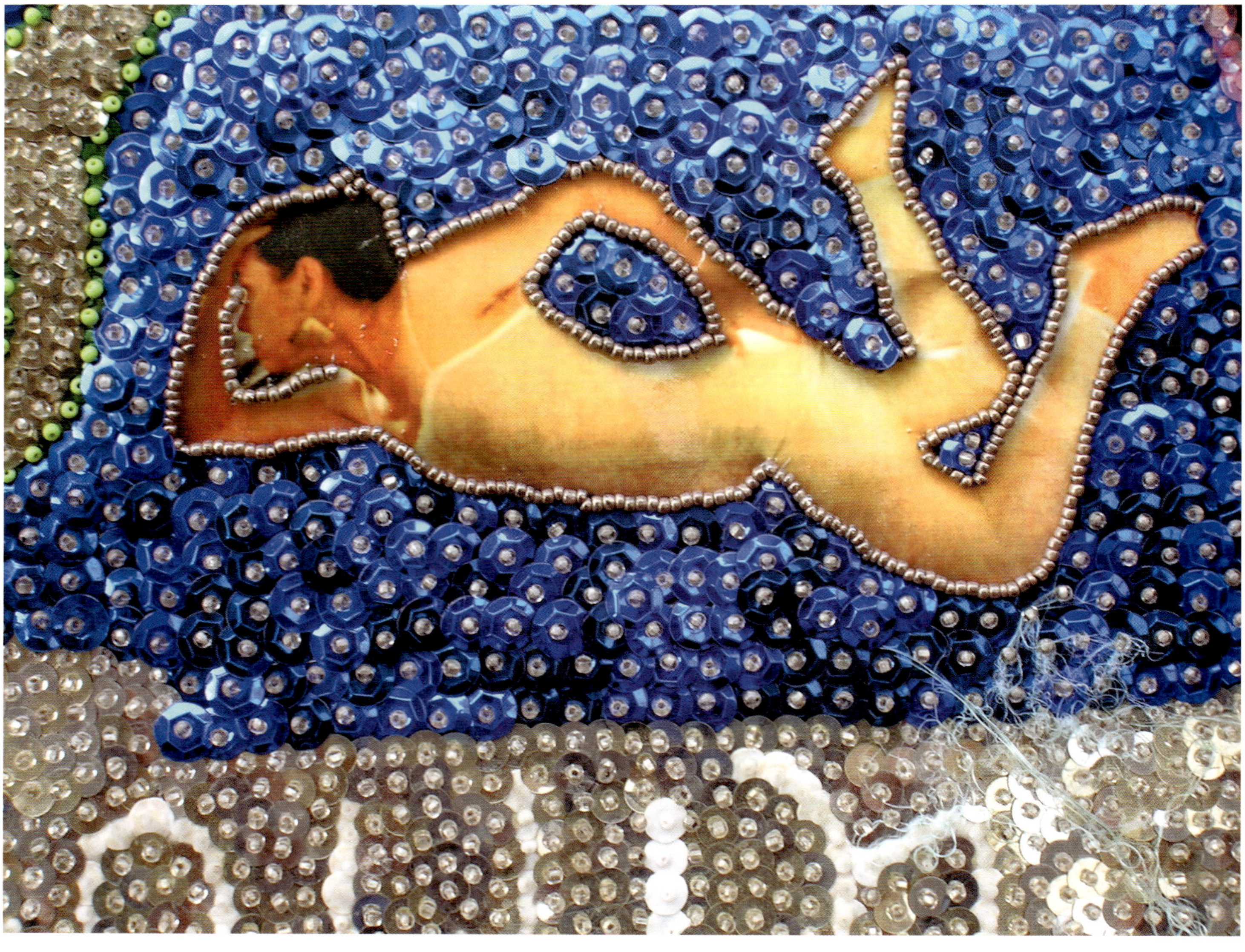

Tina Girouard is "swimming" under plastic in a detail of a La Siren flag made by Ronald Gouin.
Courtesy of Dr. Jacques Bartoli
Photo by Nancy Josephson

In 1990 Tina Girouard came to Haiti with her husband. She parked at the Oloffson (the magical Oloffson). At that time, Antoine's atelier was set up in the courtyard of the hotel. Tina (who had been told about a wonderful artist who had set up shop at the hotel, but had dismissed the idea that a good artist would be based in a hotel) noticed some activity and went over to check it out. Antoine greeted Jacques, who had brought Tina to the hotel, warmly.

According to Jacques, Tina had an instant connection with Antoine. "My eyeballs popped out onto the floor," said Tina in a interview. "Our language was always about art. The first words I learned in Creole were the different colors and payette (sequin). With Antoine and me it was all about the art." Tina sees her main contributions in simple but elemental terms. She made it profoundly clear that she viewed the flag makers as artists. She encouraged them to sign their work. If an artist brought a flag up to "Lakou Bartoli," the workshop she set up in Jacques' compound, without a signature, she would give them sequins and beads and ask that they sign the piece. "The most miraculous thing I did was keep coming back."

Within a short time Tina invited Antoine to participate in the next Lafayette festival, which would be held in April 1991. Once again the struggle to secure documents and make travel arrangements fell on Jacques along with Tina. Thankfully, they were successful.

Antoine went to Louisiana with a very large quantity of flags. Nearly all of them sold. Needless to say, Antoine came back to Haiti in fine shape financially and emotionally. Also during his time in Lafayette, he and Tina decided that Tina would come back to Haiti and collaborate with Antoine.

Tina came in 1991, just after the fall of Aristide. This trying time didn't overshadow the incredible work the two artists did together. Tina would work during the day with Antoine and stay in Jacques' compound in the evening. Jacques would drive her to work every day. During the course of this time Jacques' curiosity was piqued. Tina encouraged Jacques to buy Antoine's flags. Jacques remembers a specific flag, one in which a houngan was bending over the top of a drum in ceremony as the one that first "touched" him. This began his burgeoning collection. Meanwhile the relationship artistically and emotionally between the two artists grew.

Djab (mischievous creature) with brule zin (flaming cauldron) by Antoine Oleyant. Multi-colored background and many symbols around the central image make this flag have tremendous visual impact and movement.
Marilyn Houlberg Collection
Photo by Nancy Josephson

Antoine Oleyant

Antoine Oleyant was born September 16, 1955, in a town in the south of Haiti. He moved to Port au Prince in the early 1970s seeking a better life than the rural one he left behind. He made a living carving wood and selling to tourists in the plaza near the Musee D'Art Haitien. Since he also had access to flags and flag makers and saw that they were selling, he took the opportunity to make some extra money by selling flags as well. He was encouraged to continue with the flags by Sondra Thomas and Pierre Monosiet, who were at the Musee. Over the course of time Antoine developed his own style of flag making. Previously the flags (even the ones meant for the tourist/art market) used a standard formula in the Bel Air style. Although Antoine also used central imagery and veves in the typical style, he began using scenes in the Vodou ceremony as subject matter. He would incorporate figures, saints, offerings, veves, and other ritual objects to create a narrative that showed the power of the ceremony and the saints being depicted. He worked with what were essentially collage techniques to piece together this vibrant story. Figures and images danced across the picture plane. Sometimes he would not even use a border to hold his figures in. It would seem as if the fabric couldn't contain these images and they were bursting out of the limited field. Nobody had done this before, using the medium as a storytelling device. Antoine was the first. This was his genius.

Rather than use beads to outline his figures, Antoine just used the sequins, allowing the change of colors to indicate where one figure ends and another begins. Hand dyed sequins had been used in Haiti for some time. The dye was readily available, but it took the knowledge of how to "fix" the dye so that the color would attach to the plastic sequin to be able to utilize this material properly. Even once the knowledge was obtained and used (urea is the fixative), the non-lightfast nature of the dye on plastic compromises the pieces' longevity. The color fades over time. Antoine, however, used this to his artistic advantage, adding another tonal element into his repertoire. He used the contrast of the home dyed, more muted sequins as a background and used the more vibrant color saturated store-bought sequins as the foreground. This hue difference, which also had a sense of textural difference, really made the figures jump off the surface.

His figures have stylized forms featuring large, triangular-shaped heads with eyes close together. The boxy bodies are, despite their visual weight, surprisingly vivid, filled with life and movement. The feet of his figures feature spiky toes that turn up and give a playful undertone to the sometimes serious or tragic subject matter. His work with Tina took his initial impetus, utilizing collage ideas, and expanded it dramatically. The stories he was able to tell in a larger format (sometimes as big as fourteen plus feet) incorporated a mélange of imagery, both spiritual and political. Given the climate at the time, this was very brave.

It was suggested to Antoine by Tina that he use plastic rice bags rather than burlap to give support to the back of the flags. This simple innovation allows the flags to have a longer life due to the fact that burlap, which was used as coffee bean bags, begins to decompose due to its acid content while the plastic is physically stable. It was also suggested by Tina that Antoine may want to utilize the leftover sequins by mixing them up on the surface of one or more of the areas that were looked at as an area for solid colors only.

The success Antoine garnered was due to the wonderful collision of fate. Sandra Thomas, Maggie Steber, Richard Morse, Jacques Bartoli, and most importantly, Tina Girouard saw in Antoine an inspired artist. This support and encouragement allowed his genius to blossom. His creativity and willingness to push the boundaries in a medium that was just beginning to gain interest suggests an inspired artistic rebel. This sensibility paid off for him in his being able to further his artistic visions with the additional support, both financially and artistically, of Tina. Their collaboration allowed both to grow as artists while producing treasures that set the bar for other artists. Antoine's success was not lost on the flag makers who were working at the same time and later. His innovations were copied (still by some such as his brother-in-law, Maxon Scylla) and, with some success, pushed even further by those who followed.

In 1992 Antoine died at the age of thirty-eight. Prior to his death, Antione created a series of smaller flags in which he attempted to work out his illness. He had stopped going to a Western doctor and instead chose the use the herbal and spiritual healing found in Vodou. Many of these flags were dedicated to Baron, the spirit that is the healer and overseer of the area between this world and the next. Some of the flags were self-portraits done with the gut wrenching iconography of a body compromised with pain and confusion.

At the time of his death Antoine was the best-known flag maker of his day, employing over twenty sewers in his atelier. He is credited as the artist who took the sacred art of flag making and catapulted it into a worldwide art market. Antoine's brother-in-law, Maxon Scylla, now heads the workshop and produces a version of the master's designs.

Drummer in ceremony by Antoine Oleyant. The gorgeous green snake and purple "veve-ed" vestment are wonderful elements of this flag.
From the collection of Laurie Beasley, Ridge Art
Photo by Nancy Josephson

Antoine Oleyant flag featuring many different spirit iconographies such as swords for Ogoun, macoute (straw bag) for Azaka, cross for Guede, and snake for Damballah.
Collection of Dr. Jacques Bartoli courtesy of Nancy Forrest
Photo by Carson Zullinger

Ogoun (primary) flag by Antoine Oleyant. Note the multi-colored sequins used in the background and in some figural elements.
Collection of Dr. Jacques Bartoli courtesy of Nancy Forrest

Antoine Oleyant flag featuring iconographies from many different lwa. A lighter color palette makes this figure less ominous.
Marilyn Houlberg Collection
Photo by Nancy Josephson

La Siren by Antoine Oleyant.
The signature curled hairstyle of Antoine's La Siren has the effect of being at once humorous and fierce.
Courtesy of Tony Fisher and Devi Cholet of Indigo Arts Gallery
Photo by Carson Zullinger

Baron by Antoine Oleyant.
This flag suggests a Guede ceremony in progress, with severed limbs adding to the collaged narrative.
From the collection of Dr. Jacques Bartoli courtesy of Laurie Beasley, Ridge Art
Photo by Nancy Josephson

La Siren by Antoine Oleyant.
Here Antoine shows La Siren holding her emblems, a horn and comb. Her fish "vestment" and spikes around her body give this flag graphic punch.
From the collection of Dr. Jacques Bartoli courtesy of Laurie Beasley, Ridge Art
Photo by Nancy Josephson

Erzulie veve flag by Antoine Oleyant.
Very few flag makers could capture the simple beauty and power of the veve as well as Antoine.
Courtesy of Waterloo Center for the Arts
Waterloo, Iowa
Caribbean/Haitian Collection

Capalou by Antoine Oleyant.
This early flag suggests where Antoine is heading in later flags, with its use of various symbols surrounding the central image. Also the variegated tail feathers speak to future use of multi-colored sequins.
Courtesy of Dr. Jacques Bartoli
Photo by Nancy Josephson

Veve for Tous Les Saints (All the Saints) by Antoine Oleyant.
Here Antoine incorporates many different symbols to represent his version of Minocan.
From the collection of Dr. Jacques Bartoli
courtesy of Laurie Beasley, Ridge Art
Photo by Nancy Josephson

Ibo by Antoine Oleyant.
This flag is for one of the nations (nanchon) of Vodou families that have their roots in West Africa.
From the collection of Dr. Jacques Bartoli courtesy of Laurie Beasley, Ridge Art
Photo by Nancy Josephson

Bossou and Damballah with Guede face by Antoine Oleyant.
Antoine's flags have power along with movement. Note the legs on the snake on the right.
From the collection of Dr. Jacques Bartoli courtesy of Laurie Beasley, Ridge Art
Photo by Nancy Josephson

Double Bossou and Damballah by Antoine Oleyant.
Antoine's use of hand dyed sequins in this flag's background make the forefront figures that much more dramatic.
Marilyn Houlberg Collection
Photo by Nancy Josephson

Bossou flag by Antoine Oleyant.
Thi bull's head image with three eyes, snakes, and flag along with candles suggest strength and power through ceremony.
Collection of Dr. Jacques Bartoli courtesy of Nancy Forrest
Photo by Carson Zullinger

Two heads with legged snake by Antoine Oleyant.
The different eyes and teeth for the bottom figure and disembodied arm and leg tell a story that has overtones of Guede and djabs (mischief making spirits).
From the collection of Dr. Jacques Bartoli courtesy of Laurie Beasley, Ridge Art
Photo by Nancy Josephson

Damballah with figure by Antoine Oleyant.
The multi-colored, multi-legged snake squeezes the central figure, whose eyes are filled with snake imagery.
Courtesy of Dr. Jacques Bartoli
Photo by Nancy Josephson

Antoine Oleyant flag featuring a bold assortment of spiritual iconography which is most fiercely shown in the two crossed swords, which reference Ogoun.
From the collection of Dr. Jacques Bartoli courtesy of Laurie Beasley, Ridge Art
Photo by Nancy Josephson

Baron by Antoine Oleyant.
Guede's cross is flanked by two figures with ceremonial implements in hand.
Collection of Dr. Jacques Bartoli courtesy of Nancy Forrest
Photo by Carson Zullinger

Cross for Guede by Antoine Oleyant.
This flag features two figures who may be twins as well as priest and priestess of Vodou. Note the male figure "palming" the head of a naked smaller figure.
Collection of Dr. Jacques Bartoli courtesy of Nancy Forrest
Photo by Carson Zullinger

Carrefour Legba/Baron by Antoine Oleyant. Carrefour is the crossroads. Legba is the spirit who holds the key to the door between the spirit and secular worlds. This flag has symbols for all the spirits imprinted on its busy surface.
From the collection of Dr. Jacques Bartoli courtesy of Laurie Beasley, Ridge Art
Photo by Nancy Josephson

Antoine's beaded signature.
Note the use of the less opaque, muted, hand dyed sequins allowing the store bought sequins' vibrancy to act as a powerful foreground texture.
From the collection of Dr. Jacques Bartoli courtesy of Laurie Beasley, Ridge Art
Photo by Nancy Josephson

Djab with brule zin (mischievous spirit with flaming cauldron) by Antoine Oleyant. Surrounding the central figure is a background with "pwen" or power point symbols shown here as black line "star" motifs.
Marilyn Houlberg Collection
Photo by Nancy Josephson

Winged Spirit with Heart by Antoine Oleyant.
This incredibly powerful imagery is an Antoine piece as good as it gets.
Marilyn Houlberg Collection
Photo by Nancy Josephson

The Next Wave

Eveland Lalanne

Eveland Lalanne (1939-2003) also ranked as one of the most talented innovators of the new wave of flag makers Tall, willowy, and elegant, his demeanor mirrored his work. His distinctive use of materials complemented the iconography that sprang from his boundless creative ingenuity. Lalanne's inner light and humor shone in all his interactions, both personal and professional. From an interview, Jacques Bartoli remembers seeing Lalanne flags, "Every small patch was different from another patch. It was like a mosaic with different patterns. Together they created an image that was visible and figurative. It was really different, unexpected. He used all kinds of materials. He was not into tradition, he was going wild, though he didn't seem to be wild."

His exuberance made his work jump off the picture plane. Jewelry items that embellish his female lwas' forms are sewn so as to literally drip off their bodies: necklaces, bracelets, bejeweled gauntlets, and rings cascade from the figures. Lalanne's unusual choice of a bugle bead (much longer than the traditional seed bead) gives the impression of a frosty, muted background. He would use multi-colored sequins of varying sizes in his border work. He would frequently use a diamond pattern as an inner border prior to depicting the central subject of the flag. Only then would he let his spirit come to life. When he did, he accomplished this with a joyful display with full on fervor. The area that the lwa inhabit is pushed to the limits of the available fabric. They are very present in both physical and psychological senses. His spirits are handled with the reverence of someone who knows them well enough to play with them. The characters in Lalanne's world include evening-gloved mermaids with Wonder Woman bras, floating moon-shaped heads invoking the spirit of Baron Lacroix (guardian of the cemetery), and a kneeling shepherd next to a lamb sporting glasses (Ti Jean Petro, a warm spirit identified with St. John the Baptist). When he's "on," he's "on." His incredibly tight beaded embellishments are rendered with such a sense of devotion for the spirits, who he so dearly loves.

Eveland Lalanne.
Photo by Marilyn Houlberg

Stylistically, Lalanne uses larger "E-beads" or "6-0s" (the bead size) to "draw" the various features he needs to make stand out. Beaded noses that also go into the eyebrows are a common feature in his lwa's faces. He would not use the large beads, however, to outline the shapes of the color fields as many other flag makers do. The almond-shaped eyes are outlined in sequins of another color, making them visually a prominent feature of the flags. I was told Lalanne learned to sew flags while working in the Dominican Republic, which accounts for his use of Spanish in identifying some of the spirits he depicts (St. Jorge rather than St. George).

In his later years Eveland stopped designing new flags, but his many workshop artisans were able to copy his designs. Today these are available for sale by artists/artisans, Lafleur, Jean-Baptiste, and sometimes Lalanne's wife, Claudette (who is now sewing her own name onto the flags). One will see in the many copies subtle changes that speak to the hands and eyes of flag makers attempting to make their own statements within the confines of what the market will bare.

Erzulie Freda by Eveland Lalanne. This extraordinary flag shows all the best of Lalanne's work: facial features outlined in larger beads, muted background using longer "bugle" beads, and exquisite seed bead work using the standard chromolithograph image. *Courtesy of Dr. Jacques Bartoli* *Photo by Nancy Josephson*

Detail of Erzulie Freda by Eveland Lalanne. Note the Saint's beautifully rendered crown and halo as well as the earrings that come off of the flag's surface.

La Siren Labaleine by Eveland Lalanne.
This flag has La Siren in a Wonderwoman bra and long evening gloves. Here Lalanne uses hand dyed sequins along with store bought to play with the palette.
Courtesy of the author
Photo by Carson Zullinger

Tijan Pero (Ti Jean Petro) by Eveland Lalanne.
This was most likely done by one of the workers Lalanne employed. The charm lies in the odd "glasses on the sheep." 18" x 20"
Private Collection
Photo by Carson Zullinger

Bossou by Eveland Lalanne.
This piece is replete with all the elements of a ceremony for the spirit of the earth.
Marilyn Houlberg Collection
Photo by Nancy Josephson

Saint Jorge (George) by Eveland Lalanne.
Lalanne used the Spanish spelling frequently because he learned his trade in the Dominican Republic. This image is taken from the chromolithograph but depicts Lalanne's personal spin on the subject matter.
Marilyn Houlberg Collection
Photo by Nancy Josephson

Manman Marie by Eveland Lalanne.
"Mother Mary" is surrounded by Lalanne's angels.
Courtesy of Ted Frankel of Sideshow and Uncle Fun
Photo by Carson Zullinger

La Siren by Eveland Lalanne.
It is thought that Lalanne saw a painting of La Siren with black and white horizontal striped hair and incorporated it into his design work.
Private Collection
Photo by Carson Zullinger

Erzulie Freda by Eveland Lalanne.
This flag has Freda's jewelry literally dripping off the surface. The background, with its use of the larger tube "bugle" beads, lets the foreground figure take center stage.
Courtesy of the author
Photo by Carson Zullinger

Baron LaCroix by Eveland Lalanne.
In this version the intense blue background allows the white skeleton heads to visually jump off the surface of the flag.
Marilyn Houlberg Collection
Photo by Nancy Josephson

Baron LaCroix by Lalane.
The Baron of the Cross is a Guede spirit here depicted as floating skeleton heads.
Marilyn Houlberg Collection
Photo by Nancy Josephson

Saint Jacques Mager (Major) by Eveland Lalanne.
This flag is Lalanne's design brought to life by his wife, Claudette. Lalanne had many in his atelier who continue on using their teacher's designs.
Courtesy of Maggie Roche, Edge Art
Photo by Nancy Josephson

Marinette by Claudette Lalanne.
Here Eveland's wife, Claudette, shows Eveland's influence over her design concept.
Marilyn Houlberg Collection
Photo by Nancy Josephson

Yves Thelemaque

Yves Thelemaque (also written as Telemac or Telemak) was born February 9, 1955, in Port au Prince. His father, Emmanuelle Andre Thelemaque (nicknamed Weweet), was a famous houngan in the Bel Air section of the city. Among others initiated by Weweet was Boss To. During the time Boss To was studying with Weweet, he was also using the temple grounds to make flags for those mambo and houngans. Additionally, during the busy season before Rara he was working on commissioned costumes for as many as six different Rara groups.

Yves attended school erratically due to financial problems. He wanted to be a car mechanic. During the early 1970s he was exposed to and learned the techniques used in flag making. Yves became one of Boss To's assistants when needed. In about 1976 he went to work in the Rawlings baseball factory, operating some of the machinery. He worked at the factory for eight years until he and others asked for a raise and were fired. During this time, on weekends, he would assist Boss To in the costume and flag making work.

For six months after he was fired Yves didn't have a direction. Then a houngan came to him with a flag order. With the consent of Boss To, Yves took the commission. The first flag he made was a traditional one just like the one's Boss To was making. Since this was to be a ceremonial piece, it was made using a heavily sequined border with an interior that was very lightly sequined so that the flag had an unfettered sway during the course of its use. More commissions followed. Boss To had suggested that in order to give the flags a richer look nicer material such as satin or velvet should be used for the interior part of the flag that was left bare. It was suggested to Yves to try to sell his flags at either the galleries that were in town (Marassa and Monin), and that he might have luck selling to Sondra Thomas at the Musee. He was encouraged as sales increased.

About two years into his new business, Yves began experimenting with the form. The borders of the old flags had been made using solid sequined patterning. These border elements then became fair game for Yves.

As the borders developed, so did interest in buying flags made by Yves. He viewed each piece as needing a different border treatment. This border patterning idea became his trademark. The borders were striking in that they were wide and full of movement. They were (and are) outlined with larger beads with varying colors, filling in each of these outlined areas. He made the interior design primarily from Bel Air stencils that many of the flag makers used and shared.

Yves consigned one of his pieces to another flag maker. This artist sold the flag, declaring that he was its maker. The buyer wanted the artist to make another flag just like the one he had bought. When the artist attempted to copy Yves work, he failed miserably. Weweet got news of this and went to Yves with the suggestion that Yves sign the flag

Yves Thelemaque.
Photo by Nancy Josephson

Yves Thelemaque with flag in process.
Photo by Ted Frankel

Saint Jacques Majeur/Ogoun by Yves Thelemaque.
This rendering of Ogoun features a newer concept using the circle to enclose the central figure. This makes for a more visually flowing flag.
Courtesy of Ted Frankel of Sideshow and Uncle Fun
Photo by Carson Zullinger

somehow to avoid a repeat of this unhappy occurrence. Yves began identifying his flags by adding in sequins "Y.T."

It took years before Yves would smile at me. I wasn't sure whether he didn't like foreigners in general or me specifically. After finally inadvertently cracking whatever code needed to be cracked, or merely because I kept showing up and finally wore him down, his reticence to interact slowly evaporated as I realized his reserved nature was actually based in his shyness. Normally one would expect Yves to follow in his father's very large footsteps, but it's hard to know Yves and think of him as having the type of character that would enable him to be comfortable forging such a public life. His confidence seems to lie in his work, bold and clear, defined and sharp. The sometimes-formulaic interior is mitigated by the extraordinary work holding the piece together. All of his work has a tight, professional look. The outlined images are expertly crafted. He is a stickler for this professional look and will not abide by sloppy work done by anyone in his atelier. He is also not happy to see other work that he feels doesn't carry his high standards of craftsmanship. When he saw a flag I had bought from another flag maker with the satin border basted on instead of finished properly, he took the flag out of my hand and brought it back the next day beautifully finished.

Erzulie Freda by Yves Thelemaque. Yves uses the chromolithograph as a jumping off point for this tightly rendered flag. Freda's face is sequined with much smaller (5mm) sequins. Note the use of Yves' trademarks, including the playing card suites indicating divination.
Courtesy of Kurk Lyons
Photo by Carson Zullinger

Saint Pierre by Yves Thelemaque. Legba in the body of Saint Peter is the spirit being honored in this flag. Here note the folds in the figure's garment expertly wrought using larger beads as the outline.
Courtesy of Kurk Lyons
Photo by Carson Zullinger

Erzulie Dantor by Yves Thelemaque.
The beautiful border and encircled spirit keeps this flag visually vibrant.
Courtesy of Kurk Lyons
Photo by Carson Zullinger

Detail of Erzulie Dantor by Yves Thelemaque.
Note the larger beads used to outline Yves' version of Dantor.

Erzulie Dantor by Yves Thelemaque.
Here Yves uses the chromolithograph as a jumping off point for a strong graphic statement. The black pig is a favorite offering for this tough spirit.
Marilyn Houlberg Collection
Photo by Nancy Josephson

Erzulie Dantor by Yves Thelemaque.
Here is a different version of one of Yves most successful interpretations of Dantor, featuring the spirit surrounded by many of the objects used in ceremonies in which she is honored.
Courtesy of Waterloo Center for the Arts
Waterloo, Iowa
Caribbean/Haitian Collection

Claire Mesine by Yves Thelemaque.
This flag for Claire Mesine or Saint Claire is a tribute to the spirit who helps obtain clarity. The pineapple is normally a symbol associated with Dantor, whose crown has the appearance of the top leaves of the pineapple.
Marilyn Houlberg Collection
Photo by Nancy Josephson

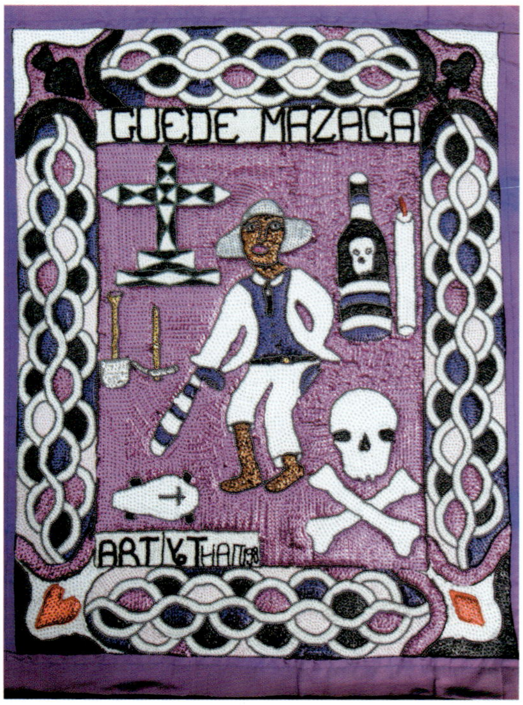

Guede Mazaca by Yves Thelemaque.
In this flag the three colors most associated with the Guede spirit, purple (here shown as more pink), white, and black, are utilized to show the spirit with some of the objects that he uses during a ceremony.
Marilyn Houlberg Collection
Photo by Nancy Josephson

Gran Bois Ile by Yves Thelemaque.
The half man, half tree spirit is another favorite theme of Yves'. Healing leaves are used as great design elements.
Courtesy of Dr. Jacques Bartoli
Photo by Nancy Josephson

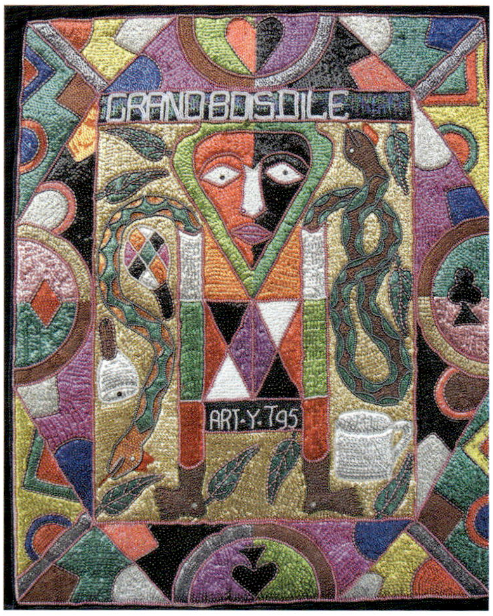

Loco Atissou by Yves Thelemaque.
Yves' depiction of a simple veve is catapulted into a different artistic realm by using strong spiritual iconography.
Courtesy of Waterloo Center for the Arts
Waterloo, Iowa
Caribbean/Haitian Collection

Simbie Anpaca by Yves Thelemaque.
This flag is expertly wrought using Yves' trademark beading outline for the veve.
Courtesy of Waterloo Center for the Arts
Waterloo, Iowa
Caribbean/Haitian Collection

Ceremonie Freda by Yves Thelemaque.
Here a veve for the goddess uses a multi-colored triangulated border to enclose the iconography. The full central field complements the dense border.
Courtesy of Ann and Ed Gessen
Photo by Carson Zullinger

Damballah Wouedo by Yves Thelemaque.
Yves' tribute to the serpent (Damballah) and his consort, Wouedo (the rainbow), shows both symbols and offerings for the spirits.
Courtesy of Waterloo Center for the Arts
Waterloo, Iowa
Caribbean/Haitian Collection

Damballah Wouedo by Yves Thelemaque. The iconography used here is true to the spiritual offerings associated with the spirits. The egg is eaten by the serpent during a ceremony. Note the different sequin colors surrounding the heart, which effectively keeps the central images from being visually static.
Marilyn Houlberg Collection
Photo by Nancy Josephson

Cermonie Dambalah by Yves Thelemaque. This flag uses another favorite set of visual information made by Yves. Here the multi-colored half circles surrounding the middle add to the quality of movement.
Courtesy of Kurk Lyons
Photo by Carson Zullinger

Damballah Wouedo by Yves Thelemaque. Yet another tribute to the life force spirits of the serpent and the rainbow.
Courtesy of Kurk Lyons
Photo by Carson Zullinger

Cermoni (e) Bossou by Yves Thelemaque.
In this flag, the central character's strength is matched by the encroaching patterned border.
Courtesy of Waterloo Center for the Arts
Waterloo, Iowa
Caribbean/Haitian Collection

Djobolo Bossou by Yves Thelemaque.
In Haiti, the ritural animal sacrifice not only is used to honor the spirit but also to feed the congregation. Here the healthy animal stands ready to be fully utilized.
Courtesy of Kurk Lyons
Photo by Carson Zullinger

La Siren Diamant (Diamond) by Yves Thelemaque.
Here Yves' depiction features the mermaid primping in the mirror with the comb thoughtfully rendered coiffing her long tresses.
Marilyn Houlberg Collection
Photo by Nancy Josephson

Diable Zenglen by Yves Thelemaque.
This strong, mischievous little devil is one of many in Yves' arsenal.
Marilyn Houlberg Collection
Photo by Nancy Josephson

La Sirene Diamant by Yves Thelemaque. All of the siren's iconography surrounds her. The addition of a leafy vine keeps this flag filled up with graphic interest and movement.
Marilyn Houlberg Collection
Photo by Nancy Josephson

Les Sirens Diamant by Yves Thelemaque. The two stylized sirens dance together on the picture plane. Note their tails incorporating border patterns.
Marilyn Houlberg Collection
Photo by Nancy Josephson

La Siren in trance by Yves Thelemaque.
This mermaid is depicted deep in trance, as suggested by her large eyes.
Marilyn Houlberg Collection
Photo by Nancy Josephson

Yves remembers seeing flags that had the borders extend all the way into the central image. Though it is difficult to anticipate or predict what Yves' next artistic step will be, during this conversation I saw Yves mulling over this idea. He sees the work of an artist as constantly moving forward to the next idea. His will be an interesting career to watch as it goes forward, since he is already considered to be a master in this field. Yves' work continues to be a sought out by collectors and connoisseurs of th e medium. He is recognized as a maverick in the medium and as such commands respect in the field. His work is featured in museums around the world that show and value the art of Haiti.

Old flag by unknown maker.
Here is a flag with the borders coming all the way in to the central image. Yves suggested this might be an idea for his next progression.
Marilyn Houlberg Collection
Photo by Nancy Josephson

Roland Rockville

Roland Rockville was born May 3, 1954, in the outskirts of the beautiful seaside town of Jacmel and came to Port au Prince in 1957. He went to primary and secondary school. His work is special, inspired. He truly is an artist through and through. Of all the sequin artists, Roro is the only one who has had any drawing experience in an academic setting. When he was twelve years old he remembers meeting Serge Charlotin at school. Serge, a painter, saw Roro's drawing of Erzulie Dantor. From Serge, Roro learned painting at the famous Centre d'Art. The Centre d'Art was an art center that was started by Dewitt Peters, an American schoolteacher and artist who saw Haitian art and was inspired to create a center that would act as a place where Haitians might be able to get art lessons and sell in the gallery space as well. From the ages of twelve to twenty, Roro sold paintings and made murals for street stores and borlettes (lottery booths). Additionally, he painted murals in the temples that would hire him. Unfortunately, he became allergic to the paints that he used, so at twenty he decided to learn plumbing, electrical, and welding trades at a vocational school. He didn't spend a long time at these trades. The lure of making art drew him back to his first love.

He had learned the art from a neighbor and fellow artist, Clotaire Bazile, for whom he sewed and drew designs. He ended up managing the atelier since Clotaire was splitting his time between Port au Prince and Miami. He had interactions with Sondra Thomas at the Musee gift shop and remembers Oldoff and Antoine from this time. He remembers Oldoff was selling pens and Antoine was selling wooden sculpture to tourists on the plaza outside the Musee. Oldoff was just learning how to make flags from the only female artists working at that time, Mdme. Polonne and Monique. Their styles were not particularly dramatic, so Roro advised Oldoff on how to make his flags more appealing. Roro also advised Antoine on his art and technique.

Roland Rockville.
Photo by Nancy Josephson

In 1981, Roro decided to utilize his artistic skills in a way that was safer for him than painting had been. Since he had experience in Clotaire's atelier, he decided to open his own in this year. He worked simultaneously at the Centre d'Education Special teaching painting and sewing to disabled children and teens.

Roro brings a painterly style that innovatively uses the limited color palette of sequins to give a three-dimensional quality to his work. His knowledge of perspective and tone is expertly crafted into deeply spiritual narratives. Roro's most effective pieces involve intricate stories of lwa interacting with earthly concerns. He enlists the spirits' help to tell fables with clear messages, many of which are cautionary tales showing the consequences of bad decisions. In an amazing display of knowledge of material and medium, Roro uses a variable color combination of seed beads and sequins to incorporate shading into his work. His fully formed figures are the polar opposite of most sequin artists' stylized imagery. Roro values his originality, viewing each flag as a piece unto itself. They are not, as he puts it, "Like a bunch of mangoes." He considers perspective the alpha and omega of a flag. "You have to show where you're coming from and where you're going."

Roro's style is so dramatically his own, so distinctive in imagery and use of materials. His commitment to the spirits is borne out in all he does. He went through the grueling process of reaching the next level of his spiritual path. In July 2004, Roro became a houngan. Without a doubt his additional spiritual knowledge has added to his fantastic creative impulse.

La Sirene by Roland Rockville.
This is an early Rockville that was made prior to his adding his signature. The flag has a Gaugin quality to it.
Courtesy of the author
Photo by Carson Zullinger

Erzulie Freda by Roland Rockville.
In this small flag (14" x 14"), Roro utilizes the chromolithograph as the underlay for some serious embellishment.
Private Collection
Photo by Carson Zullinger

Papa Damballah by Roland Rockville.
Here Roro uses other elements, including mirrors, to work out his vision of veve-like iconography.
Private Collection
Photo by Carson Zullinger

Erzulie Dantor by Roland Rockville.
Roro's Dantor uses the chromolithograph as a starting point. The tremendous use of different sequins in the same color family to depict a shaded more three-dimensional idea is Roro's ultimate signature.
Private Collection
Photo by Carson Zullingerb

Siren, Agwe, and Freda by Roland Rockville.
This large flag features a wide array of spirit and offering iconography all see by the seaside.
Courtesy of Dr. Jacques Bartoli
Photo by Nancy Josephson

Santa Marta chromolithograph.

Erzulie La Flambo by Roland Rockville.
This hot version of Erzulie uses the chromolithograph to start. The foreshortening on Erzulie is a little off, but the shading on her robe and body are spot on.
Courtesy of the author
Photo by Carson Zullinger

Reception La Siren by Roland Rockville. This luncheon served around the pool is a fabulous tribute to Roro's love of the spirit. All of the mermaids wear jewelry that hangs off the surface of the flag.
Courtesy of the author
Photo by Carson Zullinger

Detail of Reception La Siren by Roland Rockville. Plastic is used over food and drink offerings. Roro and I worked on several flags together where the idea of the plastic overlay was explored.

Deesse(?) de la Foret by Roland Rockville.
La Siren cavorts in a forest stream in this narrative. The "cord" she is holding is actually a snake being lovingly kissed by the mermaid. Elephants, zebras, rhinos, and leopards add to the scene.
Private Collection
Photo by Carson Zullinger

La Reine by Roland Rockville.
"The Queen" of the mermaid is entangled with Damballah, whose crown connotes his royal standing as well.
Marilyn Houlberg Collection
Photo by Nancy Josephson

Madan Gran Bwa by Roland Rockville.
This active narrative shows the forest spirit in another form.
Courtesy of Ted Frankel of Sideshow and Uncle Fun
Photo by Carson Zullinger

La Siren by Roland Rockville.
The small (5mm) sequins make expert use of the detail needed in this 13" x 13" flag depicting a relaxed mermaid comfortably overlooking her realm.
Private Collection
Photo by Carson Zullinger

Maitre Gran Bois by Roland Rockville.
Here a chromolithograph inspired Saint Sebastian image is coupled with a more traditional version of the tree/forest spirit.
Courtesy of Dr. Jacques Bartoli
Photo by Nancy Josephson

Detail of previous Rockville flag.
Here Roro's King of Kings is nourishing the Damballah life force.

Flag by Roland Rockville.
This flag incorporates all of Roro's vivid imagery, iconography, and narrative as well as his unbelievable technical skill.
Courtesy of Dr. Jacques Bartoli
Photo by Nancy Josephson

Guede Mazaka by Roland Rockville.
This flag is not only visually stunning in it's iconography, but the incredible color sense and technical prowess is a tour de force for the maker.
Marilyn Houlberg Collection
Photo by Nancy Josephson

Brave Guede by Roland Rockville.
Rockville's art background is evident here in his ability to use perspective, indicating depth of field.
Marilyn Houlberg Collection
Photo by Nancy Josephson

Detail of Guede Mazaka by Roland Rockville.
Note the fabulous beadwork and use of alternative materials to add to Roro's arsenal.

Baron by Roland Rockville.
In this narrative, the spirits are unwilling to release the newly deceased body, feeling that those who may abuse the life force don't understand the goodness of the life recently departed.
Courtesy of the author
Photo by Carson Zullinger

Guede by Roland Rockville.
This flag utilizes Roro's skills to show a beautifully rendered skeleton along with perspective, shading, and narrative.
Private Collection
Photo by Carson Zullinger

In 2005, Roro was terribly burned by oil during a ceremony in Port au Prince. Though he is recuperating, he is severely compromised and cannot use his arms and hands properly. He has made at least one flag since the accident, which is shown here.

Roro and I have an interesting relationship, one that borders on familial. I became the godmother for one of his sons, Junior. I have worked with Roro on many projects that challenge both of us. He has tried to have me open the "Atelier Josephson-Rockville" for many years. Whenever I need to rely on someone to understand how I approach my sequin work, I look to Roro. We fight, laugh, and create what I feel is wonderful work together. I respect his artistic aesthetics deeply even as I am challenged by some of his choices. My association with Roro has powerfully influenced my artwork, and I see some of his art being influenced by my work.

Reine La Diablesse by Roland Rockville.
The Devil Queen flag is the first flag Roro completed after his accident.
Marilyn Houlberg Collection
Photo by Nancy Josephson

Roro's wife, Mona, is a beautiful woman with a big, easy laugh. She has put up with Roro through all of his escapades. She is nursing him back to life through this difficult period. She is also making her own flags in her own voice. For a long time she helped Roro by sewing his designs. She is now developing her own style, which incorporates some of Roro's figure rendering skills with more stylized free-flowing imagery.

Marassa Toire (Trois or Twa) by Mona Rockville.
Roro's wife, Mona, is beginning to develop her own style, drawing from her husband's references but using a more stylized figure.
Marilyn Houlberg Collection
Photo by Nancy Josephson

Marinette by Mona Rockville.
Mona's quirky flags are a wonderful combination of figural interpretation and studied technique. She is a force to be looking at for the future of the art form.
Marilyn Houlberg Collection
Photo by Nancy Josephson

Ronald Gouin

Ronald Gouin was born in Fond de Neg near Aux Cayes on December 8, 1969. He moved to Port au Prince, into a neighborhood near Antoine Oleyant. He worked in Antoine's smaller atelier in the early 1980s. He was still in primary school at the time and learned drawing and coloring ideas in school. He continued to work at Antoine's atelier until, in 1985, an argument over finances made Gouin leave. He put his own frame together and drew a flag design, Baron Cimitre. He bought sequins from the Iron Market and produced his own first piece, which sold immediately.

Brash, ex-body builder Gouin exudes self-confidence in a larger than life way. His work echoes his manner. Frequently his signature on a flag is equal to or larger in size than the name of the spirit depicted. The surface of his flags can barely contain the images. It feels as if the story told is continued past the picture plane. The energy within the borders has a pulse that speaks to Gouin's keen innate ability to combine texture using anything around him to create a visually electric surface. He used larger 20mm sequins (known as embargo sequins) to help cover the surface and fill up space at a time when the US embargo made acquiring the 8mm sequins extremely difficult. He used tiny sequins. He used large plastic beads. He used anything that was available to get his work done. Stylistically his figures are reminiscent of Antoine's oddly boxy images with pointy toes.

It has been a while since I have seen a new flag by Gouin. He still makes beautiful sequined libation bottles for the tourist trade, but I miss his energetic portrayals of narratives that have spark and life. Gouin's wife, Jean Carline, is now the flag maker in the family. Gouin is trying to educate himself so that he and Jean Carline can better their conditions.

Ceremonie Cadia Bossou by Ronald Gouin.
This large flag (32" x 64") incorporates many Vodou elements beautifully while deeply referencing Antoine's influence. Gouin worked at Antoine's atelier prior to his going out on his own.
Courtesy of Dr. Jacques Bartoli
Photo by Nancy Josephsonb

Azaka by Ronald Gouin.
The figure of the spirit, along with the veve and other iconographic images, show Gouin's work in a relatively subdued mode here.
Courtesy of Dr. Jacques Bartoli
Photo by Nancy Josephson

Bossou by Ronald Gouin.
Gouin does not reference any spirits but signs the piece boldly.
Courtesy of Dr. Jacques Bartoli
Photo by Nancy Josephson

Azaka Medhe by Ronald Gouin.
The stylized figure and Vodou offerings for the farmer (Azaka) are only kept in place by the triangle border.
Courtesy of Dr. Jacques Bartoli
Photo by Nancy Josephson

Flag by Ronald Gouin.
The bent over figure filled with veves can barely be contained in the picture plane.
Courtesy of Dr. Jacques Bartoli
Photo by Nancy Josephson

Ceremoni by Ronald Gouin.
This flag featuring a ceremony for the dead has powerful symbolism coupled with defined yet personal forms.
Courtesy of Ann and Ed Gessen
Photo by Carson Zullinger

Damballah by Ronald Gouin.
Here Gouin has strong connections between Damballah, the life force, and Guede (casket depiction), whose realm is the next world.
Courtesy of Ann and Ed Gessen
Photo by Carson Zullinger

Damballa et Erzulie by Ronald Gouin.
This is truly a unique flag based on Gouin's personal assessment of the spirits involved.
Courtesy of Dr. Jacques Bartoli
Photo by Nancy Josephson

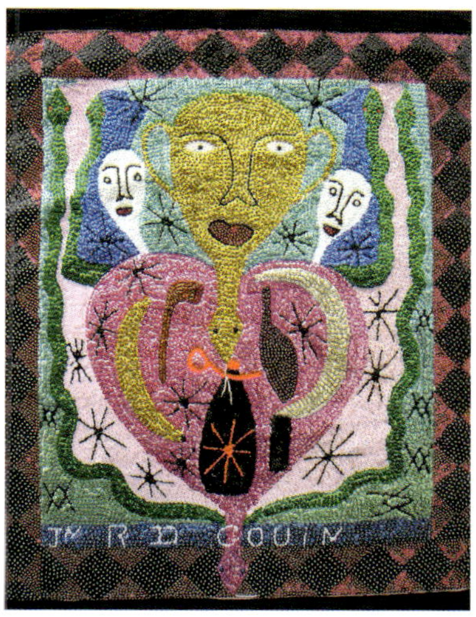

Flag by Ronald Gouin.
This flag features the heart, referencing Erzulie, snakes (Damballah), as well as many "pwen" (power points).
Courtesy of Dr. Jacques Bartoli
Photo by Nancy Josephson

Ceremonie Legba by Ronald Gouin.
Legba stands at the crossroads between sacred and secular worlds as well as earthly and afterlife worlds. Here Gouin deals with all of these aspects.
Courtesy of Ann and Ed Gessen
Photo by Carson Zullinger

Double Bossou by Ronald Gouin.
This piece is reminiscent of Antoine's artwork, but with Gouin's twist. Note the snake on the left sprouting legs.
Marilyn Houlberg Collection
Photo by Nancy Josephson

Dambala by Ronald Gouin.
The spirit of the life force is incorporated into a flag featuring many other Vodou related elements, including the horizontal figure seeming to be entombed. The dramatic black "X" cutting through the center of the flag adds another layered dimension to the piece.
Courtesy of Dr. Jacques Bartoli
Photo by Nancy Josephson

La Sireine by Ronald Gouin.
The possible misspelling of La Siren is perhaps a reference to the queen of the sea (reine). Here a photo of Tina Girouard swimming along under the watchful eye of the mermaid spirit is an additional surprising element.
Courtesy of Dr. Jacques Bartoli
Photo by Nancy Josephson

Georges Valris

Georges Valris was born in October 1950 in Cavaillion. He came to Port au Prince in 1950 and worked as a basket maker. He never liked working for other people and aspired to starting his own business one day. After he left basket making, he took a job in sewing in a clothing factory. He worked there for an additional five years until slowdowns in production caused him to leave. His knowledge of English and his educated background allowed him to get a job as a stevedore on a cruise ship. He saved enough money over the years to follow his initial dream of opening his own business. A friend of Georges (Niemois) had shown Georges the sequin sewing technique and in 1988 Georges opened his atelier and made his first flag. He went to the Iron Market to get sequins and material. His first flag was a heart (Erzulie's symbol). He took it to Gallery Marassa, where it was purchased. The second piece took longer to sell, but eventually tourists and galleries bought all the subsequent work. Georges was in business. Georges was also selling to Jacques Bartoli, who recognized in Georges a serious businessman.

Georges Valris eschews the title artist. Instead he prefers to be known as an artisan. He recognizes and relishes his position as one of the few flag makers that tightly control their own atelier. He values his reputation as a "go-to" guy that will "get the job done." He has done sequin flag work for other artists (Allison Sayre, Tina Girouard, and others) and more recently Eduard Duval Carrie, who commissioned Georges to produce flags using Carrie's images. These flags were featured in an exhibition at the UCLA Fowler Museum of Cultural History. His craftsmanship and business-like approach to work are highly prized in a place where there is every possibility that the piece commissioned will be sold to the first person that comes along with interest and cash.

Georges' flags, however, do possess a consistent, recognizable hand that distinguishes his work from others. He fills any background empty space "voids" with arching multicolored rainbows, fish, and other objects that make for a visually tightly packed flag. The cartoon-like features of his figures have a distinct quality. The figures have a goofy, strong presence. Even in his serious statements there is a light, almost humorous visual language speaking loud and clear.

Though Georges makes Vodou flags, he is adamant about his faith, which lies in the Catholic religion. He makes Vodou flags because, "When people come to Haiti they want Vodou flags." Georges sees no discord between making flags for a religion that the Catholic Church does not value and seeing himself as a deeply committed Catholic.

In 1992, after the death of Antoine, Georges began working with Tina, who had been introduced to Georges by Jacques. He became the director of her atelier. Their association proved particularly rich for Georges in that the inspiration for many of the images he continues to use come from this early liaison. This notion mirrors the concept of syncretizing Catholic images into Vodou iconography. Cross-pollinization lives in all sorts of forms in Haiti.

Georges Valris.
Photo by Marilyn Houlberg

La Siren by Georges Valris.
This flag shows the typical format of Georges' work with a strong central figure (here with some serious eyelashes) surrounded by smaller trademark elements such as rainbow half circles, fish, and stars.
Courtesy of the author
Photo by Carson Zullinger

La Siren by Georges Valris.
In work I had done with Georges, there was one design that he sewed using references found in this piece. The oversized tail may be Georges' sense of humor.
Courtesy of Tony Fisher and Devi Cholet of Indigo Arts Gallery
Photo by Carson Zullinger

La Siren by Georges Valris.
This version of La Siren looks as if she is ready to spring off the fabric.
Courtesy of Anne Josephson
Photo by Carson Zullinger

Erzulie Dantor by Georges Valris.
The tiny hands of the Madonna are standard in Georges' vocabulary. This flag shows Dantor's solid strength.
Courtesy of Tony Fisher and Devi Cholet of Indigo Arts Gallery
Photo by Carson Zullinger

La Siren and Consort by Georges Valris.
This colorful flag has loads of life and movement.
Courtesy of Karyl Weber and Grant Folin
Photo by Carson Zullinger

Flag by Georges Valris.
Here Georges' work with Tina shows with the use of collage techniques along with political overtones.
Courtesy of Ted Frankel of Sideshow and Uncle Fun
Photo by Carson Zullinger

Skeleton by Georges Valris.
In Georges' interpretation of Tina's designs, he brings his own color sensibility to this lively flag.
Marilyn Houlberg Collection
Photo by Nancy Josephson

Cross by Georges Valris.
Skulls, snakes, and candles dance while the heavy cross of Guede anchors everything into place.
Marilyn Houlberg Collection
Photo by Nancy Josephson

Cross by Georges Valris.
Here once again Tina's influence is interpreted by Georges, who uses much Vodou iconography in his work. Though he is a devout Catholic, he says, "People want Vodou flags."
Courtesy of Ted Frankel of Sideshow and Uncle Fun
Photo by Carson Zullinger

Skull by Georges Valris.
This striking rendition of an image and iconography captures the raw energy of Guede.
Marilyn Houlberg Collection
Photo by Nancy Josephson

Flag by Georges Valris.
This older flag by Valris uses hand dyed sequins in a piece chock full of political imagery. The rooster symbolizes the Aristide party.
From the collection of Laurie Beasley, Ridge Art
Photo by Nancy Josephson

Bossou by Georges Valris.
Georges explains that in this piece the bull represents Haiti, the calf Haiti's children, and the udders are "fraternite, equalite, and liberte de Haiti."
Marilyn Houlberg Collection
Photo by Nancy Josephson

Georges' wife, Andremise Brianvil, is using the new beading style born out of the wedding dress factory technique to create her own style of flags. Georges' son, Valentine, is continuing on in his father's atelier, producing some very distinctive work of his own when not in school. Georges is encouraging both.

Andremise Brianvil.
Photo by Ted Frankel

Saint Jacques/Ogoun by Andremise Brianvil.
Using the chromolithograph image, Brianvil employs a method to bead this piece learned at one of the wedding dress factories.
Marilyn Houlberg Collection
Photo by Nancy Josephson

Detail of Brianvil flag.

Gran Bwa by Andremise Brianvil.
The color choice and striking use of beads and sequins make this piece stunning.
Private Collection
Photo by Carson Zullinger

Jesus in the sun's rays by Valentin Valris.
Valentin uses techniques learned while working for his father, Georges, to work on a fully realized composition of his own.
Private Collection
Photo by Carson Zullinger

Adan et Eve by Valentin Valris.
Using Bible stories rather than Vodou imagery is part of Valentin's visual vocabulary.
Private Collection
Photo by Carson Zullinger

The Little Mermaid by Valentin Valris.
Initially commissioned, this icon is now incorporated into the Valris atelier as a pemanent fixture depicting La Siren.
Courtesy of Dr. Jacques Bartoli
Photo by Nancy Josephson

Lherison Debreus

Lherison Debreus (also spelled Debrise) was born in 1971 near the second largest city in Haiti, Cap Haitien. His mother left for Port au Prince when he was little and settled in the Bel Air area near Tibout's house and temple. When he was fourteen, Lherison joined his mother. He would hang out at Tibout's temple, which bustled with activity. He claims Tibout as his spiritual father. He also is Tibout's grandnephew by blood. When Lherison came to meet me at the Oloffson, Richard Morse, manager of the hotel, was there. When I told Richard that Lherison claimed Tibout as his granduncle, Richard had no trouble believing this statement. His is a strong family resemblance.

Lherison remembers the Rara costumes being made in the temple. Rara groups from the provinces outside the city would order costumes from Tibout. Lherison began participating in the atelier work, which included flag making.

In 1994, Tibout died. Lherison was on his own. He decided to continue making flags. Also, he stepped up his activity of scouring the countryside looking to buy sacred objects that he could sell in Port au Prince. He combined this business with another in which he acted as an agent for some of the sculptors who worked in the Iron Market. The famous artist, Pierrot Barra, was one whose work Lherison would sell to buyers, including Jacques.

Sometime around 2002, Lherison came to Jacques with a beautiful textile that he claimed was an old flag from a temple. The flag featured stuffed beaded work that Jacques had seen done on older Rara costumes. Jacques also had some older flags with hints of this same beadwork. The flag appeared old. It was dirty and had burn marks indicating its use in ceremony. Lherison sold it to Jacque as an older flag that he had found while scouring the countryside for sacred objects to purchase.

Though this was a very beautiful object, it was not old. The giveaway was that it had been clearly made on the frame to which it was still attached. The fabric border that was integral to the piece needed the rigid frame. There was no way it could have come off the frame and kept it's form. In ceremony the flag needs to flow and be waved as flags are meant to do. If this had been used in a ceremonial way, it would have knocked someone over due to its stiff, heavy construction. It is common knowledge that a sacred older object will bring more money than a new piece, so Lherison decided to put some age on his work. Frequently, "antiqued" flags and other cult objects are sold in the market, where their value is considered higher than contemporary work. When confronted, Lherison expressed no remorse for having sold this piece, knowing its age, but he did say he had some pieces that he had not "antiqued." Most were smaller sized pieces, which made them more manageable weight- and bulk-wise.

Technically, Lherison's flags are made up of two pieces of material with a design drawn onto the top fabric. The design outline is sewn through the two layers of material. Small cuts in the back fabric are made and cotton stuffing is pushed through the two layers. This forms a three-dimensional puffed image on the front of the piece. The top is then embellished with rows of beads to cover the stuffed images. Sequins are sewn in a scattered design around the central figure.

This stuffing technique, known in old European textile production as trapunto, is coupled with beading techniques that are reminiscent of West African beadwork. That it had been used in older flags in a much more limited version, and that it translated to the Rara costumes that had been made in Tibout's atelier, is an interesting historical side note.

That Lherison made the transition from techniques that were known, but used in relatively insignificant ways to amplify them to make his own unique pieces is inspired. His market driven urge to age the work is an ongoing issue. When not "antiqued," these pieces stand on their own (almost literally) as strong artistic statements steeped in an updated version of ancient Vodou traditions. He has successfully expanded an old idea to fit a contemporary art market.

Lherison Debreuse.
Photo by Nancy Josephson

La Siren by Lherison Debreuse.
The larger than normal flag (24" x 48") uses the stuffed "trapunto" technique to achieve its 3-D characteristics.
Private Collection
Photo by Carson Zullinger

Baron by Lherison Debreuse.
The chromolithograph of Saint Gerard is used to depict the Vodou spirit Baron, one of the Guede family.
Courtesy of the author
Photo by Carson Zullinger

Back of the Baron flag by Lherison Debreuse.
The small cuts made into the back of the doubled fabric get cotton stuffing, which makes the top of the flag not only 3-D, but also very heavy.

La Sirene by Lherison Debreuse. The design on the front of this flag is put on before stuffing is inserted through the back. Here the mermaid is stuffed and ready to be beaded.
Courtesy of Laurie Carmadie, Gallerie Bonheur
Photo by Nancy Josephson

Finished piece by Lherison Debreuse.

Siren by Lherison Debreuse.
The variegated tale of the mermaid adds to the visual beauty. Feet coming out from the tail references the mermaid's other life.
Private Collection
Photo by Carson Zullinger

Erzulie Freda Heart by Lherison Debreuse. This puffed veve is a stunning example of the simplicity of symbol holding tremendous power.
Courtesy of Laurie Carmadie, Gallerie Bonheur
Photo by Carson Zullinger

Legba Atibon by Lherison Debreuse. Here Lherison uses the Saint Lazarus chromolithograph to identify the central figure, then surround him with Vodou iconography including asson and cloche (rattle and bell) used to "call" the spirits.
Private Collection
Photo by Carson Zullinger

Jan Zonbi by Lherison Debreuse.
This depiction of a cemetery scene shows a deeply held Vodou narrative. Note Lherison's initials and identification of the title are done with beads that read as stripes. This is done by putting two colors of beads that alternate with each other: 1 red, 1 white, 1 red, etc.
Courtesy of Ann and Ed Gessen
Photo by Carson Zullinger

Clair Mezin by Lherison Debreuse.
Santa Clara or Saint Claire's image is used as directly as possible in this flag.
Marilyn Houlberg Collection
Photo by Nancy Josephson

Wagler Vitale

Wagler Vitale was born in Aux Cayes February 21, 1959. He came to Port au Prince in 1981. He liked to draw as a child but received no formal training. Still, his talent developed. His skills in the construction field have enabled him to keep a level of employment cherished in Haiti, where the unemployment rate is seventy percent. However, his first love is painting.

When he was younger (in his early twenties) he met a neighbor, Burton Chenet, who is a well-known and very talented painter. Burton encouraged Wagler after seeing his paintings. Burton supplied Wagler with materials that are always in short supply. Wagler was successful in selling his paintings to several galleries around Port au Prince and the more upscale suburb, Petionville.

In the early 1990s he began making flags after meeting another neighbor, Petit Frere Mogirus. Initially, Wagler just drew the designs for Mogirus, who had previously kept his flags simple. Wagler's designs translated well to the new medium. The successful partnership blossomed, with Wagler drawing and Mogirus sewing.

Vitale's flags have a specific color palette that has the background and much of the central imagery using pale and muted sequins. Frequently, a black outline will define the images and figures. He explained that color choices were limited due to availability of sequins. He and Mogirus live on the outskirts of the flag-making scene. Though there were sequins to be bought in the Iron Market, Vitale chose to use what he could get in his neighborhood. This was a limited palette.

His imagery was based less on Vodou and more in Catholic images and parables. Unlike the Bel Air area, which is steeped in the ritual, traditional knowledge of Vodou, Vitale's neighborhood had a more democratic religious atmosphere. This he captured in his designs. As an artist, he accepts the full array of inspirations available to him whether they be Vodou or Catholic based.

Vitale's first love is painting. The unlimited arrays of color choices allow him to more fully explore the ideas he is interested in pursuing. He looks at the lack of the sequin color choice as a limitation to his work. Even though he regards his flag making as a secondary art form, his flags deliver very specific, clear massages based on a recognized repertoire of image, color palette, and execution.

Wagler Vitale.
Photo by Ted Frankel

La Sirene by Wagler Vitale.
The loopy tail of the mermaid makes for a loose and informal narrative.
Courtesy of Ann and Ed Gessen
Photo by Carson Zullinger

Bois Cayman by Wagler Vitale.
Bois Cayman is the place where the Haitian revolution began. It is said to have started in a Vodou ceremony that gave the uprising soldiers the power to go into this long struggle.
Courtesy of Dr. Jacques Bartoli
Photo by Nancy Josephson

Marrassa Trois by Wagler Vitale.
These three figures all hold objects used to call the spirits.
Courtesy of Dr. Jacques Bartoli
Photo by Nancy Josephson

Erzulie Freda by Wagler Vitale.
Erzulie's body and heart are one in Wagler's depiction of the lwa.
Courtesy of Dr. Jacques Bartoli
Photo by Nancy Josephson

Jesus on the Cross by Wagler Vitale.
Using Bible stories is an important part of Walger's visual vocabulary. He doesn't want to be tied to only one set of symbols.
Courtesy of Dr. Jacques Bartoli
Photo by Nancy Josephson

Flag by Wagler Vitale and Petite Frere Mogirus.
This collaboration is the result of a design by Wagler and construction by Mogirus.
Courtesy of Dr. Jacques Bartoli
Photo by Nancy Josephson

Story of Abraham by Wagler Vitale and Petite Frere Mogirus.
This is another collaboration between artists using biblical themes.
Courtesy of Dr. Jacques Bartoli
Photo by Nancy Josephson

Valet de Batons by Wagler Vitale.
This beautiful flag features the signature muted color palette and wavy/striped border frequently seen in Wagler's flags.
Courtesy of Dr. Jacques Bartoli
Photo by Nancy Josephson

Lionel St. Eloi

Lionel St. Eloi (born in 1950 in Port au Prince) lives in a cinder block castle he built in Port au Prince. He is famous, known primarily as a metal and mixed media sculptor and painter. He has had many exhibitions around the world and has work in museums featuring the art of Haiti. His genius knows no bounds. It was suggested to him that he try making a flag. True to form, he approached this challenge with an unbridled enthusiasm that allowed all the materials at his disposal to be used in the process. He cut plastic bottles into large circles to represent sequins. He used all sorts of different fabrics as paint. His flags have the tremendous spirit associated with the other art forms with which he is so familiar. Since he is new to the form, it will be a wild ride to see where he takes it.

La Siren by Lionel St. Eloi.
St. Eloi is known primarily for his mixed media sculpture and painting. His recent foray into the flag-making world has produced pieces that stem from his genius creativity.
Courtesy of Ann and Ed Gessen
Photo by Carson Zullinger

Gran Bois by Lionel St. Eloi.
Note the large plastic circles that reference old flags' sparse sequin placement.
Courtesy of Ann and Ed Gessen
Photo by Carson Zullinger

Papa Azaka by Lionel St. Eloi.
Lionel's version of a veve for Azaka features iconography associated with the spirit depicted and constructed in a way only Lionel could have done.
Courtesy of Ann and Ed Gessen
Photo by Carson Zullinger

And Many Others

This is by no means the only group of people using sequins to make flags. I include these men because they have made contributions to the medium that set the tone for those who follow.

The fabulous work of Jean Baptiste Jean Joseph, an artist living in Croix de Bouquet, shows power and an innovative nature. He combines sequin and bead work fluidly. In his atelier there are several workers that are beginning to shine on their own. For example, one sewer, Gabrielle, uses an undulating striped background to surround the busy iconography he sews.

Jean Baptiste Jean Joseph.
Photo by Ted Frankel

Adam and Eve by Jean Baptiste Jean Joseph.
The figures of the couple holding strategically placed leaves flank a tree with a snake, which in this case probably does not represent Damballah.
Courtesy of Maggie Roache, Edge Art
Photo by Nancy Josephson

Painted door at compound of Jean Baptiste Jean Joseph.
Croix de Bouquet, Haiti.
Photo by Ted Frankel

Opposite page, top:
Chaumeire Dambala by Jean Baptiste Jean Joseph.
This church image is beaded with sequins sewn sparsely around it. The fabric that shows through is rich velvet.
Courtesy of Judy Hoffman
Photo by Carson Zullinger

Opposite page, bottom:
Ceremony by Gabriel from atelier Jean Baptiste Jean Joseph.
This flag from one of the workers in Jean Joseph's atelier leans heavily on the technique and iconography of the head artist's teaching. The variegated lines of sequins undulating off the images add an electric current feel to this flag.
Courtesy of the author
Photo by Carson Zullinger

CHAUMIERE DAMBALA

Beautiful work by others, including Reynold Cleresier, the Cherisme family, Maxon Scylla (Antoine's brother-in-law, who continues running the successful atelier by using Antoine's designs and pushing their limits), Menos, and LaFleur (who claims Lalanne as his cousin and continues using the designs inspired by Lalanne), abound.

There are so many anonymous pieces that rival those of any of the artists mentioned. In Haiti, where literacy is a major problem, writing by those who have little or no access to education is not an available skill. Communication is visual and aural, not written. In many people's minds, putting a signature on a flag doesn't give any more or less value. The designation of artistic ownership can be a fluid concept in Haiti. Once again, individuating means taking a chance and putting one's self in a potentially vulnerable position with the community. Some makers don't feel comfortable taking this tack and decide not to sign their pieces.

Whatever the reason, these flags should not be valued less because they cannot be attributed to a specific individual. Beauty and art live where they live. We do an injustice both to ourselves and the culture that creates them to classify them as less.

When flags are made using designs by others, this presents problems for collectors, gallery owners, and the outside art market in general. When Maxon interprets one of Antoine's ideas, employing his own sensibilities regarding color and material, when does it become his work? Or, should we even be thinking in terms of who is responsible for the work? In Haiti, the collective is important. The piece is born out of the cultural experience. The Western notions of categorizing art don't fully apply when looking at work made outside the strict cultural and historic Western European traditions. This issue is more keenly felt in the work of the artists using beads as their primary material.

Cermoni Bois Cayman by Menos.
This flag celebrates the ceremony that was said to have started the Haitian revolution that ultimately led to independence.
Courtesy of Dr. Jacques Bartoli
Photo by Nancy Josephson

Saint Jacques/Ogou by Dieumaitre.
This flag by the little known maker offers a simple but direct approach that still contains personal vocabulary.
Marilyn Houlberg Collection
Photo by Nancy Josephson

Saint George/Ogoun Feraille by Dieumaitre.
The wide, mostly unembellished border acts as a perfect frame for the chromolithograph-based rendition of the military spirit.
Marilyn Houlberg Collection
Photo by Nancy Josephson

Detail of Saint George/Ogoun Feraille by Dieumaitre.

Lougarou by unknown maker.
The lougarou is a nightmare producing werewolf image in Haitian cultural mythology. Here we see a ceremony featuring this devilish creature overseeing the ritual. The word "mort" (dead) is under the female horizontal figure.
Courtesy of Dr. Jacques Bartoli
Photo by Nancy Josephson

Baron by C.R.
Here is a bold statement addressing the power of the Baron Guede spirit.
Courtesy of Ted Frankel of Sideshow and Uncle Fun
Photo by Carson Zullinger

Marassa Trois by M.B.
Another Lalanne inspired flag by a former atelier worker. In this flag, the eyes of the figures start possessing a different look than that of their master's work. This interesting transition speaks to individual creativity starting to well up to push past mere imitation.
Marilyn Houlberg Collection
Photo by Nancy Josephson

Erzulie Dantor by Catile.
This is one of many Lalanne inspired flags made by former atelier workers for Lalanne.
Courtesy of Ted Frankel of Sideshow and Uncle Fun
Photo by Carson Zullinger

Djab by Maxon Scylla.
Maxon was Antoine Oleyant's brother-in-law who managed Antoine's atelier. Since Antoine's death, Maxon has been using Antoine's designs. He is, however, becoming bolder in his own design contributions.
Courtesy of Ted Frankel of Sideshow and Uncle Fun
Photo by Carson Zullinger

Flag by Maxon Scylla.
This flag uses hand-dyed sequins in the background and more opaque examples in the foreground to present a powerful graphic with an abundance of iconography.
Marilyn Houlberg Collection
Photo by Nancy Josephson

Marassa Twa by Maxon Scylla.
Maxon's version of Antoine's design employs his own sense of color along with a push towards an individual aesthetic as seen by his rendering of the figures' more rounded heads.
Courtesy of Ted Frankel of Sideshow and Uncle Fun
Photo by Carson Zullinger

Beaded Flags

A new technique in flag making showed up in the beginning of the 1990s. It was born from a technique that was used in the wedding dress factories in Port as Prince. The heavily embellished bodices of the dresses were exported to Europe and America. They featured tightly beaded swirls intertwining floral and vine designs. Occasionally sequins were put into the design as an additional textural element. These dresses were extravagant in a way that got the attention of the woman who is looking to fulfill a once in a lifetime experience. The intricate, highly decorative work is based in an old French beading technique called tambour.

The technique starts with a design drawn onto the back of a piece of fabric. This is then stretched onto a frame with the design side up. A long string of beads is held under the frame in the fingers of one hand that will "feed" the beads one at a time securely to the fabric. This underside will eventually become the front of the flag. The tambour needle is essentially a tiny, sharp crochet hook that is poked through the top of the fabric. The hook, after poking through to the underside of the fabric, then turns and grabs the string in between two beads. It is then brought back up through to the topside of the fabric. The maker positions the next bead close to where the needle's first hole was made. The needle is then poked as close as possible to the previous hole. Each time the string is caught, it is brought through the previous stitch, which locks in place the long running chain. This continual process goes on until the underside of the fabric (which will be the front of the flag) is fully covered. Though it seems counterintuitive, the part that the maker cannot see becomes the front of the finished piece. Essentially, the maker is working blind, using the outline design (which is the back side of the flag) as a guide for where the beads need to change color in order to create the design.

The wedding dress factories have since closed down, but their legacy leaves behind the knowledge of something learned being transformed into a new and vital art form. Since most of the factory workers were women, it is the women who are responsible for creating and producing this beautiful work.

The work being done is for the collectors and those in the art market. With the exception of one temple where they are using flags by Myrland Constant, I know of no others used in the sacred context. The weight and stiffness of the fully beaded surface ensures that the ability to have these pieces as traditional, sacred flags is almost impossible.

Many designs are bought from artists (primarily painters) outside the atelier. These magical works shine brightly, no matter what the circumstances are surrounding their origin. The wonderful swirl of iridescent blue surrounding a pink and orange fish makes or breaks how a piece hangs together. The collective elements that are needed to work towards a fully realized artistic statement include incorporating a design (whether from inside or outside of the atelier), having available the beads that are needed to fabricate the piece, the knowledge of the difficult technique (and variations of the technique) used, developing a group of sewers who are proficient in the craft, aesthetic concerns of color selection, organizational skills, and marketing acumen. Additionally the head artist needs to have a strong background in the Vodou traditions represented in their work. Knowledge of what colors need to be used to depict various lwa is crucial. Understanding the interaction of the figures depicted is essential. They must be aware of not only the world of their atelier, but also the world in which they must sell their work.

The energy used to bring a flag to fruition requires the vast array of knowledge. Collective communal consciousness is the ultimate genius of these artists.

Andremise Brianvil holding the tambour needle which pokes through the design to hook the string underneath.
Photo by Nancy Josephson

Brianvil pokes through and grabs the string in between each of the beads to create a locked running stitch on top of the flag.
Photo by Nancy Josephson

View from underneath the frame.
One hand is placed underneath to "feed" the bead or sequin, placing them tightly next to each other.
Photo by Nancy Josephson

Myrlande Constant

Myrlande (known popularly as Constant) was born in Port au Prince on June 18, 1968. Her mother worked in one of the wedding dress factories. Sometimes her mother would bring piecework home with her to finish. Constant learned the technique and was able to help her mother finish the sewing. Eventually, Constant was hired to work at the factory. She remembers making butterflies and flowers. When she found out that only her mother would be paid for the work of both, she questioned this policy. She was fired. Unbeknownst to her at the time, this closed door led to an entirely new way in which the art of the flag would grow.

Soon after being fired (sometime around 1990), someone came to Constant with a picture that he wanted translated onto fabric using the technique learned from making wedding dresses. This opened up the idea for opening her own atelier. She has done some of the designing as well as relying on the drawings of artists Ti Jean (Michel Jean Claude, born in 1971), Ti Fre, and Patrick.

She is a vodouist who is knowledgeable in the traditions. She was the first to push the beaded flags out into the world. For a young woman in Haiti to accomplish what she did is genius in itself. She deserves to be recognized as the one who opened up an entire new category of artwork into the world.

Myrland Constant.
Photo by Marilyn Houlberg

Pierre Danbalah Negre by Myrand Contant.
Damballah regards his royal visage in a mirror, which reflects back a handsome human face.
Marilyn Houlberg Collection
Photo by Nancy Josephson

Still life by Myrland Constant.
29" x 32"
Courtesy of the author
Photo by Carson Zullinger

Detailed back of Pierre Danbalah Negre.

Erzulie Freda by Myrland Constant.
This larger flag (50" x 51") starts with the chromolithograph, then goes on and on with exquisite embellishments.
Courtesy of Ted Frankel of Sideshow and Uncle Fun
Photo by Carson Zullinger

Saint Michael by Myrland Constant.
This powerful colorful piece with angels is taken from a drawing Constant was given.
Courtesy of Ted Frankel of Sideshow and Uncle Fun
Photo by Carson Zullinger

Saint Nicolas by Myrland Constant.
Another beautiful adaptation of a chromolithograph with dense beadwork depicting the main character with rolling hills behind him.
Marilyn Houlberg Collection
Photo by Nancy Josephson

Detail of Saint Nicolas flag.

Damballah Wedo by Myrland Constant.
Here the mermaid and merman embrace the drum in a flag referencing ceremony. The choice of black for the background makes all the figures that much more alive.
Courtesy of the author
Photo by Carson Zullinger

Maitre Gran Bois by Myrland Constant.
This piece packs a lot into a small space (approximately 10" x 14"), showing a version of Saint Sebastion with veve in the background.
Courtesy of Tony Fisher and Devi Cholet of Indigo Arts Gallery
Photo by Carson Zullinger

Ceremony for Marinette by Myrland Constant.
The figure for the representation of the person "mounted" by Marinette is portrayed upside down coming down the central tree or Poteau mitan. This is difficult to see with the colors of the figure so close to the background color tones.
Marilyn Houlberg Collection
Photo by Nancy Josephson

Baron Samedi by Myrland Constant.
This jaunty portrayal of the Guede figure captures his character well in this flag.
Marilyn Houlberg Collection
Photo by Nancy Josephson

Ceremonie by Myrland Constant.
A wild scene is depicted in this lively flag. All the characters are wonderfully reproduced as individuals who are all combining their efforts for a communal sacred goal.
Courtesy of Waterloo Center for the Arts
Waterloo, Iowa
Caribbean/Haitian Collection

Bark Ceremony by Myrland Constant.
This scene shows the ceremony in which a structure is filled with favorite offerings for La Siren and Agwe, then taken out to the sea and sunk.
Marilyn Houlberg Collection
Photo by Nancy Josephson

Damballah Wedo by Myrland Constant. A gorgeous, large (45" x 52"), and very heavy flag shows the main figure in a Gran Bwa setting. In the last initiation rite of priesthood, the initiate goes to Gran Bwa for the final acceptance.
Courtesy of Ted Frankel of Sideshow and Uncle Fun
Photo by Carson Zullinger

Amina Simeon

Amina Simeon was born in Jacmel on March 10, 1959. Her sweet, beautiful smile mirrored her personality. She also had worked in the wedding dress factory that had previously employed Constant. Amina worked at the factory after Constant had been fired, but the two women knew each other. In 1994, when Amina was laid off at the factory (which eventually shut down completely in 1997), she began an apprenticeship in Constant's atelier. Shortly after that Aristide came back into power and tourism increased. Over the course of a short time, Amina saw that the flags on which she sewed were selling well. She knew the places where they were selling and knew to whom they were selling. At one point Amina decided to start her own atelier. I saw her flags first when drummer and educator, Franck Desire, brought them to the States. He had come to Oak Park, Illinois, for a school exchange program. He told me Amina had worked for Constant, but that she was now independent. He acted as her agent in the US. The flags he had were stunning. The level of design and craftsmanship were amazing. Each had depth with narratives, veves, and images of the lwa in chromolithograph format vying for my attention. Later I had the person who helped me negotiate my way around Haiti early on ask around to find out where Amina lived. I wanted to keep track of her work to see if the overriding quality of the individual pieces bore out over the long haul. I also want to meet her, artist to artist.

Through her I developed a working relationship with Jean Marie Bien Aime, who had been so instrumental in acting as an agent between the artists who wanted to sell around the Musee and clients who wanted to buy artwork back in the early days of art flag making. He was acting as Simeon's agent in Haiti. His expertise in the marketplace, combined with his knowledge and trustworthiness, allowed him to negotiate the fine lines that overlay all business transactions in Haiti.

Painting by Pascal Cornet, 2000.
It is difficult to say which came first, the painting or the flag design. Pascal is Myrland Constant's half brother.
Marilyn Houlberg Collection
Photo by Nancy Josephson

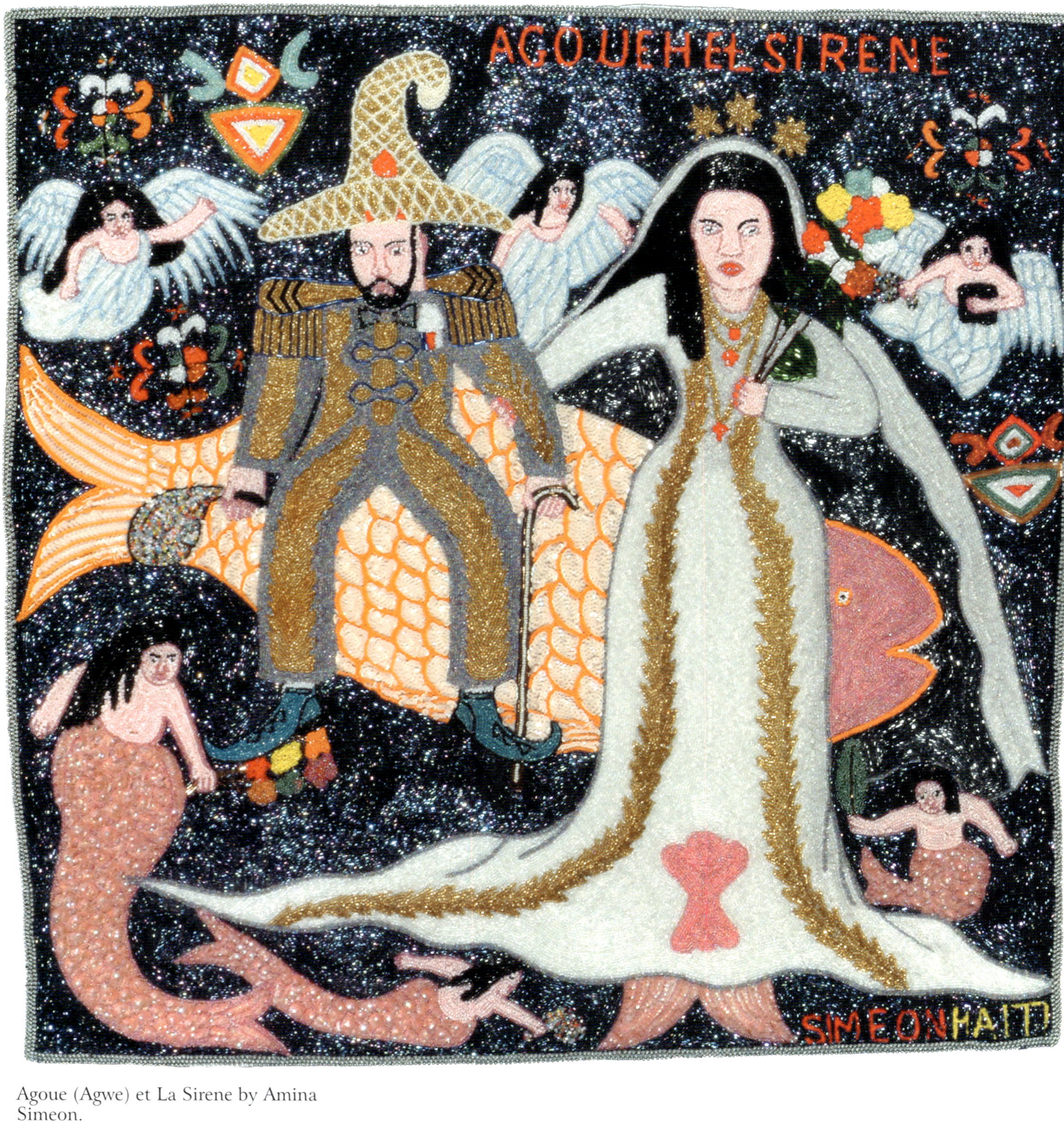

Agoue (Agwe) et La Sirene by Amina Simeon.
Several other artists have used this design as a jumping off point for individual interpretations. 32" x 32"
Courtesy of the author
Photo by Carson Zullinger

Hot in Haiti

In 2004 I went to Haiti with my son Jake and several other people. This was Jake's first time there. This was a time in Haiti where the politics were heating up. Disappointment was brewing over Aristide and his inability to fix the myriad problems keeping Haiti in such continual dire straits. We found ourselves in the middle of an increasingly unstable situation, with outbursts of gunshots surrounding where we were staying. I had been to Haiti before during some intense times of instability, but never with the level we were experiencing and not with either of my kids. The morning of the day we were supposed to fly out was particularly charged. The guns were popping rounds regularly. The smell of sulfur indicated how close we were to the eye of the storm. We all were trying to figure out how we could get out safely. I decided that we would stay until it was safe, not knowing whether that would be the next day or the next week.

Jean Marie went to see what was going on in the street. Our transportation was waiting, though the driver was not all that interested in negotiating the best route to the airport. Jean Marie came back from checking out the street. He turned to me and said, "It's time to go, Madame." He hadn't called me Madame before. For some reason this got my attention through my panic. I protested. He said, "I can't let anything happen to you. Let's go." I understood exactly what he meant. He depended on me as a source of his livelihood over the long haul. His reputation as a go-between, translator, and negotiator was at stake. His life depended on keeping us safe. We all hopped into the back of the tap-tap (a converted pick-up truck with benches in the rear) and blasted out to the airport using a series of back roads to get there. I value the relationship I have with Jean Marie on many levels. Included in this laundry list is the fact that he kept my son safe from harm.

Nancy Josephson and Jean Marie Bien Aime.
Photo by Ted Frankel

Back to Simeon

Though I now know that Ti Jean did most of her drawings, the work has so much of Simeon in it that it overshadows anything else. She also rendered images done by Andre Pierre and Burton Chenet and others. Pictures in books and art postcards were used as references. Sometimes the full design was appropriated. Other times elements of the images were picked out to combine with Amina's own design ideas. The professional way in which she controlled her atelier (which employed as many as twelve people at a time) and produced such elegant work is a tribute to her power. Her business acumen that enabled her to use the skills of Jean Marie added to her skills in the marketplace.

Amina died in 2000 of what was most likely a ruptured appendix. The story on the ground, however, varies dramatically. Most have Vodou overtones of jealousy and revenge. Some things that don't make sense, including dying before one's time, can only be dealt with by looking to the spiritual world.

Ti Jean.
Photo by Ted Frankel

Ti Jean design.
Ti Jean draws his designs on bed sheets, and then sells the pieces to various bead artists.
Photo by Ted Frankel

Amina Simeon.
Photo by Marilyn Houlberg

Amina Simeon at work.
Here Amina flips the frame so the viewer can see the beadwork in progress.
Photo by Nancy Josephson

Erzulie Freda by Amina Simeon. Amina stays close to the original chromolithograph in her depiction of the Vodou goddess of love.
Courtesy of the author
Photo by Carson Zullinger

Erzulie Dantor by Amina Simeon.
Direct use of the chromolithograph shows the various styles of the original source still making for a strong visual statement.
Private Collection
Photo by Carson Zullinger

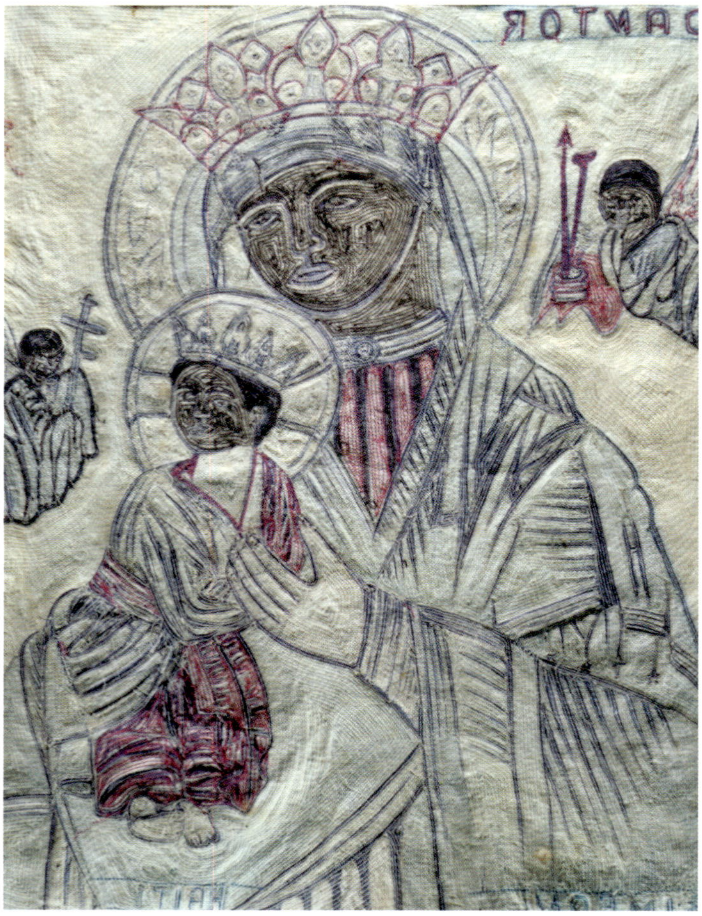

Detail of the reverse side of the previous flag by Amina Simeon.

Dantor by Amina Simeon.
Here Dantor's background is less filled up than usual. The main figure, however, presents a strong, solid representation of the earthy spirit.
Marilyn Houlberg Collection
Photo by Nancy Josephson

Baliann by Amina Simeon.
This flag is a representation of Mapiann, who is thought of a Dantor's little sister. Note the floral embellishments filling the background, referencing the patterning on the wedding dresses.
Private Collection
Photo by Carson Zullinger

Ceremonie Bak La Sirene by Amina Simeon.
Here the celebration continues for La Siren and her cohorts, who revel in the offerings sent down to them from the surface of the sea. Crabs and fish carry bowls of assorted fruits to the participants.
Courtesy of the author
Photo by Carson Zullinger

Agoueh Taworo by Amina Simeon.
The scene is joyous as many mermaids surround the strong presence of La Siren's consort, Agwe.
Private Collection
Photo by Carson Zullinger

La Siren by Amina Simeon.
Here a solid La Siren holds an asson (sacred rattle) in one hand and a mirror that captures the handsome face of her lover in the other.
Marilyn Houlberg Collection
Photo by Nancy Josephson

Azaka Medeh by Amina Simeon.
With the trademark designs of Ti Jean as underlying reference, Amina transforms the simple drawing into a commanding finished piece.
Marilyn Houlberg Collection
Photo by Nancy Josephson

Trois Rois by Amina Simeon.
Three Kings uses some of Andre Pierre's designs combined with original ideas to complete this piece.
Marilyn Houlberg Collection
Photo by Nancy Josephson

Gran Brijitte by Amina Simeon.
Amina uses Andre Pierre's design to recreate a female version of Guede.
Marilyn Houlberg Collection
Photo by Nancy Josephson

Left:
Les Barons by Amina Simeon. This large flag uses images by two painters, Andre Pierre and Burton Chenet, to represent two different views of the Guede spirit.
Marilyn Houlberg Collection
Photo by Nancy Josephson

Below, left:
Detail of the left side (Andre Pierre painting) of Les Barons flag by Amina Simeon.

Below right:
Detail of the right side (Burton Chenet painting) of Les Barons flag by Amina Simeon.

Baron LaCroix by Amina Simeon.
Courtesy of Waterloo Center for the Arts
Waterloo, Iowa
Caribbean/Haitian Collection

Lavalas flag by Amina Simeon.
Amina was commissioned to do this flag for Aristide's Lavalas party headquarters. It was never paid for, so it was sent north to join Marilyn.
Marilyn Houlberg Collection
Photo by Nancy Josephson

Mirelle Delice

Born on November 17, 1965, Mirelle Delice also worked in one of the wedding dress factories. When she left the factory, she worked for Myrlande Constant, with whom she remains on friendly terms. She left the atelier to open her own workshop. She does many of the designs herself. The stylized figures feature round heads with prominent eyes. She also uses the drawings of artists Junior and Patrick. Her trademark is the use of bugle beads (longer tube beads) as background in a herringbone pattern behind the main images.

Mirelle Delice.
Photo by Ted Frankel

Dantor Mapiang by Mirelle Delice. The chromolithograph provides the inspiration for this flag by Mirelle.
Marilyn Houlberg Collection
Photo by Nancy Josephson

Detail of Dantor Mapiang flag showing Mirelle's trademark background patterning.

Flag by Mirelle Delice.
This odd and vaguely unsettling composition shows a variety of symbols and veves surrounding the central spirit.
Courtesy of Waterloo Center for the Arts
Waterloo, Iowa
Caribbean/Haitian Collection

Dantor Mapiann by Mirelle Delice.
Here Mirelle does a richly floral robe for the spirit that references the highly embellished work done on the bodices of the wedding dresses she used to make.
Marilyn Houlberg Collection
Photo by Nancy Josephson

Reine Soleil by Mirelle Delice.
In a departure from using chromolithographs, Mirelle uses many different symbols in this piece. This is also a bit unusual in that Mirelle rarely uses a patterned border on her work.
Courtesy of Ann and Ed Gessen
Photo by Carson Zullinger

Evelyn Alcide

Evelyn Alcide was born December 4, 1969. She is a wonderful craftsman who is primarily using designs drawn by Ti Jean. Her work is at its best when done in a larger format. Though these flags weigh many pounds, their overwhelming visual appeal more than makes up for the heft.

Evelyn Alcide.
Photo by Ted Frankel

Alekba by Evelyn Alcide.
Alcide's work is best represented in a larger format where she can "spread out." In this flag (31" x 49"), Legba is referenced from the chromolithograph of Lazarus.
Courtesy of the author
Photo by Carson Zullinger

Erzulie Mapiangue by Evelyn Alcide.
This sensational version of Dantor's little sister expertly utilizes the chromolithograph imagery combined with additional symbols used in Vodou iconography.
Courtesy of Ted Frankel of Sideshow and Uncle Fun
Photo by Carson Zullinger

La Siren Matennelle by Evelyn Alcide.
Showing the maternal side of La Siren, Mother of the Sea, Alcide chooses interesting colors for the figures portrayed.
Marilyn Houlberg Collection
Photo by Nancy Josephson

Baron Criminnel by Evelyn Alcide.
The harsh Guede is a tough taskmaster in this cautionary narrative. The tombs in the background add to the solid graphic quality of this flag.
Marilyn Houlberg Collection
Photo by Nancy Josephson

Baron Brigite by Evelyn Alcide.
Male and female Guede spirits are identified in this flag.
Marilyn Houlberg Collection
Photo by Nancy Josephson

Guede Nibo by Evelyn Alcide.
A coquettish mambo, a houngan with offerings, and a strong Guede spirit inhabit this piece filled with a wide array of Vodou symbols.
Marilyn Houlberg Collection
Photo by Nancy Josephson

Mariage Agoue a La Siren by Evelyn Alcide. This is Alcide's take on a design that a number of the other bead artists have tackled.
Marilyn Houlberg Collection
Photo by Nancy Josephson

Detail of Mariage flag.

Roudy Azor

Roudy Azor is starting to take the bought (primarily from his friend, Ti Jean) drawings and "play" with them in specific ways. He is using varying colored beads as background that gives an undulating feel to them. Like Alcide, his flags are best in a larger format. The narratives are much more lively. When doing the saint's images in the larger pieces, he is able to put in more detail, incorporating floral swirls and flowing leaves to make the finished work visually powerful.

Roudy Azor and Ti Jean hold Ti Jean's ballpoint pen on bed sheet drawing that will be turned into a beaded flag by Azor.
Photo by Nancy Josephson

Roudy Azor.
Photo by Ted Frankel

Erzulie Baliann by Roudy Azor.
Expertly designed and crafted with a gorgeous sense of color makes this flag a showstopper.
Marilyn Houlberg Collection
Photo by Nancy Josephson

Erzulie Freda by Roudy Azor.
Taking the chromolithograph image as a catalyst, this piece then takes on the artist's own artistic vision.
Private Collection
Photo by Carson Zullinger

La Sirene by Roudy Azor.
The undulating beadwork outlining the figure adds a sense of movement that has tremendous visual impact.
Courtesy of Anna Greenberg and John Delicath
Photo by Carson Zullinger

Agaou Poto Coli by Roudy Azor.
This is one of a series of winged dragon spirits designed by Ti Jean and executed by Azor.
Marilyn Houlberg Collection
Photo by Nancy Josephson

Agaou Tonnerre by Roudy Azor.
Intense and malevolent in its content, this powerful flag bristles with energy.
Marilyn Houlberg Collection
Photo by Nancy Josephson

Candianhou by Roudy Azor.
This flag shows Ti Jean's design (note treatment of the cross-hatched hat) crafted well by Azor with a great color sense that effectively pushes the figures to the forefront.
Courtesy of Waterloo Center for the Arts
Waterloo, Iowa
Caribbean/Haitian Collection

Cermoni Fla Vodou Nago by Roudy Azor.
The dancing figures are set on stage (note "curtains" in upper corners), referencing the ceremony as performance art.
Marilyn Houlberg Collection
Photo by Nancy Josephson

La Sirene by Roudy Azor. This feast of the mermaids looks at both the offering ceremony (Bark de Agwe and La Siren) as well as the design for the Agwe La Siren marriage as its reference.
Marilyn Houlberg Collection
Photo by Nancy Josephson

Dambala by Roudy Azor.
Damballah transforms into a human image to address a woman in personal ritual.
Marilyn Houlberg Collection
Photo by Nancy Josephson

Bead Artists to Watch

There are several other artists who use this beading technique whose work is just starting to come into its own. Among these artists are:

EDMOND was born December 5, 1974. She worked for her half sister, Myrland Constant, for several years before going out on her own.

Edmond.
Photo by Ted Frankel

Erzulie Freda by Edmond.
Using the chrom
realm with the addition of spiritual objects such as the libation cup on the bottom righthand side.
Marilyn Houlberg Collection
Photo by Nancy Josephson

Erzulie Freda by Edmond.
Myrland Constant's half sister uses a more traditional view of Freda in this design.
Courtesy of Ted Frankel of Sideshow and Uncle Fun
Photo by Carson Zullinger

Erzulie Danthor by Edmond.
The unembellished figure and background leave the stable, unencumbered spirit solid in her presence on this flag.
Marilyn Houlberg Collection
Photo by Nancy Josephson

MADAME MOREAU worked in the wedding dress factory with Amina Simeon. When the factory closed, she went to work in Amina's atelier. When Amina died, Madame Moreau began making her own flags. Her trademark is utilizing larger bugle beads as background behind the central images. The diamond pattern is more open than the more traditional, solid background. Her son, Jean Evans Moreau (in whom she is very proud), makes the designs for her to sew.

There are any number of additional artists not featured in this overview (including such notables as Benoit and Bonhomme) who are making wonderful flags. They contribute to the growing interest that has developed using this type of flag making.

Drawing of Erzulie Freda on bed sheet by Jean Evans Moreau.
Photo by Carson Zullinger

Drawing of Erzulie Freda on paper by Jean Evans Moreau.
Photo by Carson Zullinger

Erzulie Freda by Madame Moreau. This series of three photos show the chronology of how the beaded flags get designed from start to finish.
Courtesy of the author
Photo by Carson Zullinger

Looking Back, Looking Ahead

When I look back on my experiences in Haiti, I marvel at what I've learned. The experiences, both as an artist and as an interested bystander who got caught up in the whirlwind that forever is Haiti, have changed the way I approach everything. The artists I have met have humbled me with their unstoppable vision and tenacious, audacious magic.

I can't wait to see what you all do next.

Ayibobo and all big love to my artist friends.

Glossary

asson and cloche: the rattle and bell used by the houngan or mambo to call a spirit
atelier: artist's workshop
ayibobo: hallelujah
honfour: temple
houngan: priest
kleren: Haitian moonshine or raw liquor
lakou: house or compound
lwa: spirit
mambo: priestess
peristyle: temple interior
petro: the pantheon of hotter spirits
Poteau mitan: center post found in the middle of the peristyle
pwen: star shapes in veves and in flags used as power points
rada: the pantheon of cooler spirits
reine drapo: literally "flag queen" who is in charge of using the flags in the opening of a ceremony
veve: ground drawing made by houngan or mambo to entice a spirit to join a ceremony

Recommended Reading

Art Related Reading

Aid to Artisans. *Artisans of Haiti/Aritsanat d'Haiti.* Hartford, Connecticut: Aid to Artisans, 2003.

Cosentino, Donald J., ed. *The Sacred Arts of Vodou*. Los Angeles, California: UCLA Fowler Museum of Cultural History, 1995.

Galembo, Phyllis. *Vodou, Visions and Voices of Haiti*. Berkeley, California: Ten Speed Press, 1998.

Girouard, Tina. *Sequin Artists of Haiti.* New Orleans, Louisiana: Contemporary Arts Center, 1994.

Polk, Patrick Arthur. *Haitian Vodou Flags*. Jackson, Mississippi: University of Mississippi Press, 1997.

Rodman, Selden. *Where Art is Joy*. New York: Ruggles de Latour, 1988.

Vodou Related Reading

Brown, Karen McCarthy. *Mama Lola: A Vodou Priestess in Brooklyn*. Berkeley and Los Angeles, California: University of California Press, 1991.

Dayan, Joan. *Haiti, History and the Gods*. Berkeley and Los Angeles, California: University of California Press, 1995.

Deren, Maya. *Divine Horsemen: The Living Gods of Haiti.* Kingston, New York: McPherson and Company, 1953.

Dunham, Katherine. *Island Possessed*. Chicago, Illinois: University of Chicago Press, 1969.

Gordon, Leah. *The Book of Vodou: Charms and Rituals to Empower Your Life*. Hauppaauge, New York: Barron's Educational Series, Inc., 2000.

McCalister, Elizabeth. *Rara!: Vodou, Power, and Performance in Haiti and Its Diaspora.* Berkeley and Los Angeles, California: University of California Press, 2002.

Turlington, Shannon R. *The Complete Idiot's Guide to Voodoo*. Indianapolis, Indiana: Alpha Books, n.d.

La Vieille Ferme